# Turning Your STRESS Into Strength

# Turning Your STRESS Into Strength

## Robert H. Schuller

Harvest House Publishers
Irvine, California 92614

Verses marked TLB are from **The Living Bible,** copyright 1971, Tyndale House Publishers, Wheaton, Illinois. Used by permission

Verses marked NASB are from the New American Standard Bible, copyright The Lockman Foundation 1960, 1962, 1963, 1968, 1971, 1972, 1973, 1975 and are used by permission.

TURNING YOUR STRESS INTO STRENGTH

Library of Congress Catalog Card Number 77-88865
ISBN # 0-89081-113-X

**Printed in the United States of America.**

# CONTENTS

# 1

# Turning Your STRESS Into Strength

# Turning Your Stress
# Into Strength

Stress can become the source of strength in your life!

You can turn the unwelcomed intrusions that threaten to destroy your life into tremendous possibilities for good!

*This book will show you how.*

*You can conquer stress!*

The place to discover a miracle in your life is at the point where you are experiencing the greatest stress. My confidence is based on this verse from the Bible:

"In my distress thou hast enlarged me" (Psalm 4:1 KJV).

Two young boys were raised by an alcoholic father. As they became older, they separated from that broken home and each went his own way. Some years later, a psychologist was analyzing what drunkenness does to the children in a home. In his research, one of his assistants interviewed these two men. One was a clean, sharp teetotaler, the other was a hopeless drunk like his father. The researcher asked each individually why they turned out like they did. And they both gave the same identical answer: "What else could you expect when you had a father like mine?"

It's not what happens to you in life that makes the difference. It is how you react to each circumstance you encounter that determines the results! Every human being in the same situation has the possibilities of choosing how they will react — either positively or negatively.

I happen to believe in miracles. My definition of a miracle is a beautiful act of God that intervenes in a human life to do a wonderful thing. If you want to find a miracle in your life, I suggest you start by looking for a problem. Because that is the place God wants to work in your life.

But it takes two to make a miracle. God cannot use his miracle-working power in your life if you do not have the faith to let Him work.

You remember the time Jesus left a certain city without performing any great miracles. The gospel writer said, "He could do no mighty works in this city because of their unbelief." God's power can be limited by our lack of faith. God also willingly limits his own power by His own nature. He will not force us to accept His miracles. He will not treat us like robots. But in spite of these limitations, God continues to perform marvelous works in our lives.

Many of His miracles are easy to spot. For instance, several times a year ministers from around the world gather on our church campus for a special Institute for Successful Church Leadership. Early one morning during a recent Institute, one young minister was called out of the session for an emergency telephone call. He received word that his young son had fallen into a swimming pool and was being rushed to the hospital unconscious.

This young pastor from Minnesota interrupted the seminar and asked that we pray for his son as he rushed to the hospital. Later that day, I talked with his wife and found out that the boy was unconscious when they lifted him from the pool and that X-rays at the hospital indicated there was water in his lungs. Several hours later they X-rayed his lungs again and found them clear. The doctor simply said, "It's a miracle."

What a great moment we enjoyed at the close of our Institute. During our dedication service, the father, the mother and the young boy walked to the front of the church and knelt together. There wasn't a dry eye in the whole congregation.

A young family faced tremendous stress hundreds of miles from home and friends. God met them at their point of need. In the chapters that follow, you will meet friends of mine with the same testimony under a variety of circumstances—''God helped me to turn my stress into strength!'' He is able and willing to help you.

But why is it so difficult to recognize God's miracles in our lives? We are just not sensitive enough to spot them. We are conditioned by negative vibrations in our impossibility-thinking society to look at problems and not at possibilities. After all, most of us read the newspaper. And what do we read? It's filled with bad news. What if someone published a daily newspaper that reported only the good things that happened? For one thing, no one would buy it. But it would be a massive paper. probably more than twelve inches thick, because there are so many beautiful things happening in so many lives each day!

> ''A hundred million miracles
> Are happening every day,
> But only he who has the faith
> Will see them on life's way.''

Miracles are happening all the time. If you want to spot a miracle, look for a problem, a difficulty, a mountain of stress. Because often the way God seeks to reach us is in a moment of pain. *For there is no gain without pain!* Every stress-filled situation is loaded with opportunities.

Over the years I have discovered that trouble never leaves you where it found you. It always changes you permanently. It will either make you bitter, tough, hard, cold and angry, or it will turn you into a soft, gentle, compassionate, understanding, generous human being. The choice is yours!

If you are experiencing stress today, I predict it is the beginning of a miracle. That is why God allows us to run into stress-filled situations. Sometimes He wants to slow us down. Other times He wants to change our direction. In every situation, He wants to help us become strong! For it is not the mountain of stress that counts, it's what you do with it that matters.

# 2

# Conquer the Stress of Personal Tragedy

# Conquer the Stress
# of Personal Tragedy

I want to introduce you to some friends who have turned a mountain of stress into a miracle of strength. They are practicing possibility thinkers, who know that every stress-filled situation is a miracle in the making.

Pat Shaughnessy used to pastor a small church, but in the past couple of years, his church has exploded with growth. It all started with an explosion at Los Angeles Airport, where Pat lost a leg.

*Dr. Schuller:* Why were you at Los Angeles Airport that day, Pat?

*Pat:* I was about to depart, at least I thought I was, for Seoul, South Korea. I was scheduled to be there for a thirty day preaching mission. The date was August 6th. I have a pair of cuff links that were given to me by a member of my church. Engraved on them is, "A date to remember, August 6." I wear them often, but I don't need them to remind me of that date. Twenty-five feet from where I was standing, someone had planted a dynamite bomb.

The bomb went off, and it threw me thirty feet through the air. Three people standing around me were killed. The man on my left was killed, the man in front of me was killed, and the man next to him was killed. Thirty-five other people were injured. I found myself lying on my left side on the floor. I didn't lose consciousness and I didn't go into shock, even though they had to give me eleven units of blood in the hospital.

*Dr. Schuller:* They really didn't think you would make it, did they?

*Pat:* Not really. At the airport, they said there was no hope for my life. I made it to surgery and they said there was a thirty percent chance I'd live. After surgery, they gradually reduced the odds and said I had between a forty and seventy percent chance. Several days later, the hospital spokesman used the term "miraculous" as he described my recovery to the newspapers.

I was told I would have to be in intensive care for one-and-a-half to two weeks, but I was only there for a day and a half.

*Dr. Schuller:* How did you feel during this time? Were you angry at God?

*Pat:* No, I wasn't angry. God knew the bomb was there and He knew I was there. It was not an *accident*, it was an *incident*. You see, I don't believe that accidents happen. I believe that God directs everything, and it's all for our good. God didn't hear the bomb go off and say, "Wow, what was that noise in Los Angeles?" God knew the bomb was there, and He knew I was standing there, and He was saying, "Pat, I have a wonderful, wonderful plan for you. I'm going to accelerate your ministry beyond anything you could ever dream. You're not going to like it at first, but trust me."

And through this incident God has expanded our ministry in a wonderful way. I was not the victim of that bomb blast, I was the victor!

*Dr. Schuller:* Some people are going to have difficulty believing that statement. How can you say that?

*Pat:* You see, our reaction to the stimuli of life is based on what we believe. And I believe that Jesus Christ allows everything to happen in our life for a purpose. And He can turn a mountain into a mole hill. He can move the mountain if we believe Him and trust Him. So I can thank God for that experience.

Back at the airport, I could see that my left leg had been blown open at the knee. I had six fractures in my left leg and my right leg was practically gone. I knew I was going to lose my leg even before the doctor came and told me. I remember the thought coming to me, and I almost laughed in spite of the tremendous pain.

I thought, "Pat, you don't need a right leg to preach the gospel. You never preached with your leg and you never will."

We went to the coliseum when I was first out of the hospital and I asked my wife to find out where the wheelchair parking was so we wouldn't have to walk so far. She pulled up and asked, "Where's the handicapped parking?" I said to her, "Honey, I'm not handicapped. I lost my leg, not my tongue. I can still tell people about Jesus Christ."

You know, it's been amazing. I was so excited about that trip to Korea, because I would be telling people about Jesus for thirty days straight. But as a result of this incident, I have literally talked to millions of people. I have on my right side an open door to talk about Jesus Christ to every person that I meet for the rest of my life. "What happened to your leg," they asked. "I was in a bombing," I respond. Usually they reply, "Oh, that's too bad." And I can quickly say, "No, it's not. Let me tell you what happened. Let me tell you about Jesus Christ and how he can overcome any problem in your life."

Let me say one more thing. I have a friend named Wan, from South Korea. He visited with us recently and even in Los Angeles he drives like he is still in South Korea. He turned into a one-way street and my wife told him, "Wan, you're going the wrong way on a one-way street.'' Wan looked around and said, ''It okay, we child of the King, we got the right of way!'' And that's the way I feel about life, don't you? I've got the right of way, because of Jesus Christ!

Now I want you to meet someone who is a real inspiration to me. Several years ago, this great guy was a neighbor of ours and had a dream. I want you to meet Ralph Showers.

*Ralph:* Yes, I had a childhood dream of building a ranch for handicapped people. You remember when I decided it was time to start working on my dream. I had $145.00 when we went to Arizona and found a piece of property. We got help from other people and we set about getting barbwire, posts and everything else you need to start a ranch. I found an old barn I could have for $40.00 if I'd move it off the old dairy farm.

I made the deal and set out to move the barn. Sitting on top of the roof, I moved some telephone wires and backed into 7200 volts of electricity. That electricity went through my back and came out my arms. Within a few days both my hands and my arms were amputated.

*Dr. Schuller:* Weren't you knocked unconscious?

*Ralph:* As a matter of fact, no. The electricity was rolling through my body. It's interesting how it works. It goes in this rolling motion, first very fast, and then slower and slower. And as it slows down, you feel like you're dying. But as the electricity slowed down, I had this great experience with God. I really didn't want to die and God said, "Why don't you want to die?" I told Him, "I want to build this ranch. I want to see my wife and family again. I want to live!" And God said something like, "Okay." That may not be God's exact words, but at that point the electricity stopped.

At that moment, a man came along in a dump truck. We were out on a little road in the country and he was one of the few people in that area. He maneuvered his truck and put the dump all the way up, climbed up and pulled me down. As soon as I was off the wire, the electricity came back on. I was alive! And I knew at that very moment that life was going to be exciting and that God was going to use me.

I was in the hospital two months. When I got out, a man from Phoenix asked if he could write an article about me. He did, and two weeks later, the wire services had picked up the story and newspapers across the country and magazines around the world ran the story. Within six weeks we had enough money to do what I thought was going to take six years to accomplish. We opened our ranch, Rainbow Acres, with four retarded young men and a staff of eight. We started the most exciting ministry with handicapped men and women anywhere in the world and it's a Christian home! Today we have 24 mentally retarded men and women, a staff of 18 and a piece of property worth over a half a million dollars. God really multiplied that $145.00 we started with!

*Dr. Schuller:* Tell us about some of the people in your home.

*Ralph:* David was a young man in a hospital in Northern California. He was literally "put away." He could not hear, he could not talk and we weren't really sure we could help him. Today, David runs motor driven tools, walks, talks, hears and is probably one of the most exciting young men you could ever want to meet. He's earning money and buys all his own clothes. He moves in and out of society as a human being with dignity and is just one of the products of a miracle of God.

*Dr. Schuller:* How does he earn money? Do others at your home earn money?

*Ralph:* We have several businesses on the ranch. Our goal is to be completely self-supporting. And each of the young men and women at the ranch is trained to do a job. We want them to be proud of what we have and what we are. We don't want to be on social security, welfare, government grants, or anything else. We want to walk tall! So we make Christmas cards, decoupage art work, plants, rugs and picnic tables. We're trying several other ideas. The mountains are there, and we are climbing.

*Dr. Schuller:* Tell me about your artificial hands. Did you have a problem accepting them?

*Ralph:* I call them hooks. At first they were a real challenge, but I never resented them. In the hospital, I knew they had these things and I could hardly wait to get them on and get started. I still have problems with buttons and round doorknobs. But life is too exciting to worry about those little things!

Bobbi Barras has both her arms and both her legs. In fact, she used them very nicely as a fashion model. She was successful, even though she never heard a word that was said to her.

*Dr. Schuller:* I remember seeing you do some modeling here at the church, don't I?

*Bobbi:* Yes, I did a fashion show for the women, and I used to do fashion and photography modeling.

*Dr. Schuller:* And you were incapable of hearing anything. You relied on lipreading. How old were you when you discovered you were deaf?

*Bobbi:* I was 14. Up to that time, I knew something was wrong, but I wasn't quite sure what it was. And all that time I attended public school.

*Dr. Schuller:* How did you ever do it?

*Bobbi:* I learned to read lips, mostly by watching and observing those with normal hearing. I was very fortunate to be able to teach myself this invaluable technique.

*Dr. Schuller:* You must have experienced some very difficult times in your life.

*Bobbi:* Oh yes, definitely. I had surgery one time on both my knees, and it seemed like everything hit me at one time. I could barely walk, I couldn't hear, and I was really feeling sorry for myself. A good friend gave me a copy of your book, *Move Ahead With Possibility Thinking.* As I read it, my faith was strengthened. I got myself back together again.

*Dr. Schuller:* I have an interesting question. What did your husband think about your being deaf? I mean, you told him before you were married that you couldn't hear, didn't you?

*Bobbi:* Oh no, no! He didn't ask and I didn't tell him. But I ran into trouble on our wedding night when he turned out the lights.

*Dr. Schuller:* Bobbi, you're an inspiration to all of us. You are truly an illustration that with God all things are possible.

I'm excited about another friend. Her name is Joni Eareckson and her story is tremendously exciting.

*Joni:* I wasn't always in this wheelchair, Dr. Schuller. I grew up in a very athletic, outdoors-type family. About a month after I graduated from high school, I broke my neck in a diving accident, leaving me paralyzed from the shoulder level down. I had accepted Christ through Young Life when I was a sophomore in high school. But even being a Christian, the depression, despondency and fear that I felt was overwhelming. I felt as if God had almost forsaken me. I could not understand why a loving God would allow something like this to happen to me.

I laid in that hospital bed for about a year waiting to heal from a series of long operations. During that time I had an awful lot of time to think. I laid down a challenge to God, where I said that I was going to prove Christ to be truly the Son of God or that He was nothing more than a nice, moral man who left us a good life-style to follow.

*Dr. Schuller:* How did you verbalize that challenge?

*Joni:* In my anger and in my bitterness, I said I was tired of what I thought were pat phrases and of Bible verses that weren't really relevant to me. During that time some friends came to the hospital and persistently prayed and shared with me Romans 8:28, 29 KJV: *"We know that all things work together for good to them that love God, to them who are called according to his purpose."* I slowly began to see that God could use my paralysis to develop within me the image of His Son, Jesus Christ.

*Dr. Schuller:* You almost drowned in that accident, didn't you?

*Joni:* Yes, it was shallow water, and I did a deep dive. When I struck bottom, I snapped my head back, leaving me paralyzed from about the fourth cervical level down. I held my breath and waited for my sister to pull me out of the water.

*Dr. Schuller:* Even though you're a quadra-plegic, you've developed quite a reputation as an artist.

*Joni:* Right. I cannot use my hands, and I have no wrist flection. While I was in the hospital, one of the things I had to learn was to write and type with a pencil in my mouth. I was really upset with being reduced to putting a pencil into my mouth. But after awhile I began to see that it would be a good way to express a talent that I had.

I never drew much before, but I used to watch my father. He's a professional artist. As I improved, I started signing all my pictures, Joni PTL. PTL means Praise The Lord. It was about this time that God was also strengthening my spirit and revealing to me some purposes for my accident. But as you can imagine, there are still times when I get sorely discouraged.

*Dr. Schuller:* What do you do when you get these periods of discouragement?

*Joni:* That's when I really have to trust God and take the step of faith. Just because my emotions say that I don't feel that God knows what He's doing in my life does not alter the fact that God does know what He's doing. And that's just when I have to remind myself that without Christ I am powerless to do anything.

You know, I don't have the power to face my trials with victory in and of myself. That power truly comes from the Son of God. I have a saving relationship with Jesus Christ, knowing that He's the one who has died to pay the penalty of my sins. And through that I have become powerful enough to be a child of God. Through death and resurrection, I can face my trials with victory. He's the one who sustains me and gives me courage and confidence.

*Dr. Schuller:* You had both reactions so you know what bitterness and negative emotions can do.

*Joni:* I sure do. They only get you in deeper and deeper. When I was in that hospital bed flat on my back, I was so angry against God that my bitterness was directed at everyone, even the nurses. I wasn't a pleasant person. But today, when I stop and look at what God is doing in my life now through my artwork and through this wheelchair, I get excited. My suffering has caused me to depend upon God in such an intimate way.

A special friend in my life is Mary Pruetzel. The whole world was shocked when they heard the tragic news that Freddy Prinze had died. His story is sad. But his mother's story is one of victory!

*Dr. Schuller:* Mary, you look better than the last time I saw you.

*Mary:* Yes, I feel better. The last time I saw you, you said, "Mary, stop asking why." So I stopped asking why. And the Lord has been so real and wonderful to me. It's been such a contrast to those first two weeks. During that time, all I could do was question God. Why? Why my only son? I'd just cry myself to sleep.

*Dr. Schuller:* What happened when you stopped asking questions?

*Mary:* The next morning I felt God talk to me and say, "Mary, look back." When I looked back, I saw a woman who desperately wanted a child and never had one. And then God said, "I gave you this wonderful boy for 22 years. He came to you and you loved him." And that gave me so much comfort that I feel like a new person! God has been so close to me these past weeks that I can hardly explain it. I just don't have the words to describe His love and how grateful I am. I guess I finally stopped asking and started listening. I used two-way prayer — that's how I listened.

*Dr. Schuller:* You have a beautiful accent. It sounds like a mixture of Puerto Rican and New York. Why did you leave Puerto Rico?

*Mary:* It's a long story, but I'll make it short. I was engaged for three years to a young man. On the day of our wedding, all the guests were there, but the groom never showed up. I was heartbroken. It was very difficult facing my friends in that small town.

Later, I met an American pilot in the Air Force and we fell in love. Once again, we made plans for the wedding, he bought me a beautiful ring, and invited the guests to the wedding. All my friends were there, and guess who was missing? The groom was missing! I couldn't find a hole big enough to crawl into, so I left Puerto Rico and came to New York.

*Dr. Schuller:* What did you do in New York?

*Mary:* I had fifty cents in my pocket as I walked down 12th Avenue. I saw a cross and heard people singing. I said to myself, "Well, I'll go in here." So I joined the group and started singing and having fun. There were Christians and while I was with them, my problems faded. When the collection time came, I said, "God, there isn't much I can do, so here is a quarter for you and a quarter for me. Here I am. I'm in your hands."

The next morning I took ten cents and bought a paper to find a job. I got a job designing children's clothes and worked there until I went into the hospital to have Freddy.

Two years later I went back to the same job, only the boss had died. So I decided to buy the place. It seems that ever since I gave that quarter to the Lord, I have too much. I have never lacked anything. I always have more than I need and I praise God for that.

*Dr. Schuller:* Including strength in your dark times?

*Mary:* Strength is the most wonderful thing that the Lord has given me. Right now, if it wasn't for the Lord, I would be home crying instead of praising God. I live one day at a time. I don't worry about tomorrow because tomorrow belongs to the Lord. Nothing belongs to me.

*Dr. Schuller:* Mary, you've been a real blessing to me and to many others.

Some of you have suffered a loss or are experiencing a tragedy. You may not be in a wheelchair or have lost a leg or an arm, but you're discouraged with living. You're convinced that life has been cruel to you. Maybe you don't know how to laugh anymore and you don't feel like whistling. You've lost your joy. Remember, it's how you react to your situation that determines the outcome. With God's help, you can turn tragedy into triumph, stress into strength. Look at what you have left, not at what you have lost. You will discover that God is the source of your strength and He gives you new joy!

> *For the joy of the Lord is your strength!* (Nehemiah 8:10 KJV).

# 3

# Conquer the Stress of Fatigue

# Conquer the Stress
# of Fatigue

Obviously there is a difference in energy levels from one person to another. The question is, "Why?" Part of the answer relates to our physical health, but energy is more a matter of attitude than it is of age. The Bible is filled with statements indicating that our relationship to God vitally affects our human energy output. The prophet Isaiah said,

"They that wait upon the Lord shall renew their strength,
they shall mount up with wings like eagles,
they shall run and not be weary,
they shall walk and not faint." (Isaiah 40:31 TLB).

Sometime ago, I talked with Don Sutton, the ace Los Angeles Dodger pitcher. He told me how every professional athlete looks for the edge. "Because," he said, "to really be a great success all you have to do is be just a little better than everybody else. It's that simple. All you need is the edge on the competition. And," he added, "Jesus Christ gives me the winner's edge!"

I have a few more questions for Don.

*Dr. Schuller:* Don, what keeps you going when you really get worn down?
*Don:* Well, you've heard the standard line—it seems like I've been a Christian all my life. That really fits for me because I accepted the Lord into my life when I was 8 years old. And I think being a Christian has not only assured me of life eternal, which is super, but it also assures me of a stabilizing effect in my life. You see, I have a friend that is with me everyday.

There are a lot of ups and downs in professional sports. I think I would have stayed down had I not had the presence of Jesus Christ in my life to give me a better way to accomplish things and to come out of them.

*Dr. Schuller:* Don, I recently read an article in the newspaper that quoted you as saying one of my books helped you at a difficult time in your career. Is that true?
*Don:* Yes, it is. I've read some good books that

deal with self-image, but your book, *Self Love*, was much more meaningful because it is written from a Christian standpoint. I believe the key note in these books is that you can really become what you see yourself being. But there are times when the devil can really control your thinking, so it is important to understand these principles from the perspective of what Christ has done for you. I think if you can see yourself as a successful Christian, then you're going to be successful in everything else.

*Dr. Schuller:* How has your Christian faith helped you in baseball? Does your faith help you when you're out on the pitcher's mound?

*Don:* Well, I don't really go out there expecting God to give me a season with 30 victories and no defeats. If I were to pray to win every ball game, then I would be assuming that I am smarter than God. But I do believe that my faith gives me the ability to overcome obstacles.

I went through a two month spell when I think the team forgot I existed. My contribution to the team effort was zero, except for being a highly paid cheerleader. I was in a real slump. My faith in Christ kept me going and I was able to finish the season strong.

*Dr. Schuller:* Being a member of the Los Angeles Dodgers team—I've heard of the Dodgers, even though our church is under the shadow of the Angel Stadium—what are your aspirations and dreams?

*Don:* Well, as a professional baseball player, there are still a lot of things I would like to do. But I think I have really been very fortunate in baseball. But one of the really exciting things is that I am able to stand before so many people to present the Word of God and the plan of salvation. Winning is everything and losing isn't the end of the world, for I play on another team which is even more important than the Dodgers. I am able to represent Jesus Christ.

Some people think that professional sports is an easy life. Perhaps it is for some, but for Jo Jo Starbuck, touring with the Ice Capades is a schedule that really creates fatigue.

*Dr. Schuller:* Jo Jo, you are the star of the Ice Capades. It's a joy and a delight to watch you perform. I watched you skate and said, "Isn't she fantastic? I wish I could skate like that." And my little girl said, "Well, Daddy, you always talk about possibility thinking!" It really takes years of hard work to skate like you do, doesn't it? How many Olympics were you in?

*Jo Jo:* My partner, Ken Shelley and I were in two Olympic games, five World Championships and seven National Championship competitions. It was a real thrill to skate out onto the ice at the Olympic games and stand before the TV cameras and thousands of people. We had worked six hours a day, six days a week, for thirteen years—all leading up to that one performance. And in the next five minutes of your life, you know you've got to make it! If it wasn't for the faith I have in Jesus and knowing that He is there with me and lifting me up all the time, I never could have done it!

And that's the way it has continued on with my Ice Capades career. We do a performance every night, three on Saturday and two on Sunday. Physically, it's so demanding that if I didn't know that I had the strength of Jesus inside me, I could never do it. He just seems to give me a zip and a vigor when I need it most.

*Dr. Schuller:* You've got zip and you've got vigor. And you have a special glow about you. And you get it from Jesus! I'm sure someone is thinking, "How can that make sense? How in the world can Jesus come into Jo Jo Starbuck and give her strength to skate when she should be exhausted?" And that's a good question. How *does* it work?

*Jo Jo:* That's where faith comes in, I believe. The foundation is knowing Jesus and believing all those truths that are in the Bible. But what brings it all into your life, into your body and into your being, is faith. That's what really makes it all click. When you believe in your heart, then it becomes reality.

*Dr. Schuller:* Jo Jo, we can see the difference in your face. Christ is alive in you. Keep on skating!

Probably one of the most exhausting schedules anyone can keep is running across the country as Miss America. Most of the recent Miss Americas have been Christians, and Miss America 1977 found the power of Jesus Christ gave her strength for the arduous months on the road. Dorothy Benham is from Minneapolis, Minnesota.

*Dr. Schuller:* Dorothy, I think I've written to your mother.

*Dorothy:* Probably, she watches the Hour of Power constantly. It's exciting being on the program because I've known about it for several months. When I called home, my mother was ecstatic.

*Dr. Schuller:* Tell us a little bit about your life.

*Dorothy:* I've been a Christian most of my life. There was a period of time after high school graduation where I forgot about God. All my friends were deciding their careers and I was doing the same. But I wasn't listening to God or to other people—I just wanted to do what I thought was best for me. I was very impatient and wanted things to happen immediately. But nothing turned out right.

One day I simply couldn't take it any longer. I sat down and searched within myself and decided that this wasn't the way life was meant to be. I had to allow God control over my life. I decided that you just have to give your life into God's hands because He is the one that rules your life. The only thing you can do is develop the talents He has given you and allow Him to take it from there.

*Dr. Schuller:* Did you plan on becoming Miss America?

*Dorothy:* No, that's part of the excitement of trusting God. I really didn't plan to be Miss America, it just happened. Ever since I allowed God to take control of my life, I live each day as it comes. He just takes care of everything and things have turned out beautifully. God is my daily, guiding friend.

*Dr. Schuller:* How has that helped you this past year?

*Dorothy:* As my friend, God is also the inner strength that I need. And I've needed him more this year than ever. It's quite a change to go from being a college student to being Miss America. I travel constantly and am always around people. I've traveled 20,000 miles a month this year and it gets very lonely on the road. But the Lord has been a constant friend and is always there.

*Dr. Schuller:* Tell me, why is it so many Miss America's are Christians?

*Dorothy:* I'm not sure, but I have been delighted to find among the local and national groups of the pagent, that the majority of the girls are Christians. Before the national pageant took place on TV, we all held hands and someone prayed. We became a very closely knit group and will be friends throughout our lives.

*Dr. Schuller:* I am sure of something else that you are probably too modest to say. When any person has Christ in their life, it shows in the face and in the eyes. The soul comes through and that's inner beauty.

*Dorothy:* Yes, these girls are not only attractive on the outside, they do have an inner beauty that radiates from within and that makes a person beautiful . . .

I had one Miss America confide in me and say, "I know I'm beautiful now, but what about when I get older?" I said to her, "If you keep Christ at the center of your life, you'll be as beautiful when you are 90 as you are today at 19."

Mary Kay Ash has a long way to live before she hits 90. But she's a great-grandmother and she's beautiful.

*Dr. Schuller:* Mary Kay, you are one of the most dynamic, courageous, dedicated Christian women I've met in my life. I heard you retired from business one time. How did you enjoy it?

*Mary Kay:* I had worked for twenty-five years and retired. After a month of retirement, I found I had no reason to get up in the morning. There was just nothing to do, and that really gets you down. I had formerly been so busy that there weren't enough hours in the day. But I was ready to call the mortuary across the street and tell them to come and get me.

*Dr. Schuller:* You were suffering from the fatigue of boredom. What did you do?

*Mary Kay:* I sat down at the dining room table and started to write down some ideas for a book that would help women in sales careers. It was really just something to fill the hours. I spent a couple of weeks writing down all the good things the companies that I had been with had accomplished. Then I wrote down all the problems I had encountered.

Then one day, I thought, "If you're so smart, how would you have solved those problems if you'd had the responsibility and the opportunity?" So I wrote down my solutions.

Later, I read through my notes and thought, "What a wonderful company this would make if somebody would do it." I decided it was too good an opportunity to waste, so I would put it into action!

Of course, all I had was a marketing plan. Now I needed a product. I decided on a cosmetic plan and was ready to go. I took all the retirement money I had and started putting the plan into operation. My husband was to be the administrator because I didn't know a thing about administration — still don't. Together, we were a team. I handled the sales and everything related to selling. My husband understood buying supplies and how to price the product to keep us from going broke.

One month to the day before we were to open our doors, we were sitting at the breakfast table and my husband suddenly died of a heart attack.

I had half a company! Should I go on? Should I go back to work for someone else?

*Dr. Schuller:* Isn't that when your young sons came into business with you?

*Mary Kay:* I have two sons and a daughter. The day after the funeral as we sat in the living room, they said, "Mother, we think you can do anything in the world you ever wanted to do." So with that encouragement, we decided to go for "broke" and start the company.

Our first decision was that God was going to be our partner. Then we established a basic company principle which says, "Get your life in order: God first, Family second, Job third." I'm probably the only chairman of the board in the country who tells you to put your job third. I acknowledge I know nothing about men, Dr. Schuller, but I know lots about women. And this principle "frees" our women.

*Dr. Schuller:* How did business go at the beginning?

*Mary Kay:* We started with nine people. I think they were really waiting to see how fast we would fall on our faces. But my two sons were a great inspiration to me. As a matter of fact, they were the only two people I could find who would work for $250.00 a month. I soon realized that when God closes a door, He always opens a window. And the window came in the form of my twenty-year old son. How would you like to go into business with your son as administrator of everything you have in the world?

*Dr. Schuller:* How many people are involved with Mary Kay Cosmetics today?

*Mary Kay:* We have over 38,000, with almost 900 managing directors and 17 national sales directors. Last year we did a little over 90 million dollars in retail sales. For a great-grandmother, that's good!

*Dr. Schuller:* Mary Kay, where do you get the energy to run such a huge business?

*Mary Kay:* I love Jesus Christ. I've known Him since I was seven. He's wonderful.

Do you want energy? Do you want to overcome the fatigue that follows stress? I've discovered that energy comes from both the positive and the negative wires. But the negative form of energy causes a person to pull away from anything that might be difficult. Some of these people use this energy to resist God. The result is that God stays away and they stay tired.

You don't have to be a professional athlete, Miss America or Chairman of the Board to experience the stress of fatigue. But each of these people have found that *great activity is not caused by great energy, but great activity produces great energy!*

If you want the energy of God in your life, invite Jesus Christ to come into the center of your being. You'll find that you'll be in tune with an infinite cosmic source of unending, unlimited energy that will recycle itself as you do His happy work!

> *"God gives power to the tired and worn out, and strength to the weak"* (Isaiah 40:29 TLB).

# 4

# Conquer the Stress of Sickness

# Conquer the
# Stress of Sickness

One of the most difficult stress-producing problems anyone can face is chronic sickness. It is so easy to become bitter and cynical. Yet even the stress of illness can be conquered.

One of my special friends is David Nelson. When he was in high school, he became afflicted with a disease that deteriorated his body. The prognosis was that the disease would gradually get worse. He was told that he would never finish high school, since he was unable to walk anymore, and was put in a wheelchair. His classmates, motivated by his courage, decided to help him. They carried him in his wheelchair up the steps into his classrooms. His graduation became a goal for the entire school.

When June arrived, there was David in his

cap and gown with the other graduates. When his name was called out for his diploma, two of the football players picked him up, wheelchair and all, and carried him up the steps onto the platform. As he received his diploma, the whole class stood and cheered, as if they were saying, "We did it, David, didn't we!"

I would have liked to interview David, but only those who know him well can catch all of his words. So I am going to interview him through the eyes and heart of his older brother, Erick. Erick is a recording artist and even wrote a special song dedicated to his younger brother.

*Dr. Schuller:* Erick, when did David first know he was ill?

*Erick:* It actually started when he was in junior high school. He started to lose his vision at night. Then he got tunnel vision. As time went on his eyes got worse until he could see only shadows.

He was always kind of little—you know, skinny and feisty. But in high school, he just kept getting weaker and weaker. Everyone would say to him, "Why can't you do this like your big brother Erick can?" I was class president and voted most likely to succeed, but when I graduated I didn't get a standing ovation. My mother was the only one that clapped. But at David's graduation, the whole auditorium stood and applauded.

After graduation, we took him to a lot of

doctors, but no one could tell us what was wrong. They said his muscles were deteriorating and so was the nervous system, but we already knew that. They still really don't know what to do to help him. Several times he was supposed to die. In fact, once I made all the funeral arrangements, but he disappointed everyone by staying around.

*Dr. Schuller:* The first time I met David was after I received a letter from him. He wrote with huge letters. I remember he wasn't supposed to live very long then. But a lot of people prayed and it is a miracle he is still alive today.

*Erick:* A lot of people know that it is a miracle he is alive today. I used to pray with David and run him around to prayer meetings all over. He would get mad at me because he didn't want to feel weird and have people praying over him. Then it got down to the point where he couldn't move or anything. I was in his room and I knew he didn't want me to pray for him, so I didn't. At least, I didn't pray out loud. But I said to him, "David, all you can do is talk to God right now, so why don't you do that." He said, "Okay." It seemed he improved from that point on. That's when he started watching the Hour of Power.

*Dr. Schuller:* Did that help?

*Erik:* Well, he saw—he really didn't see much on the screen—and heard you talking about life and power and hope and that there is an answer to the problems in life. And he wouldn't believe me when I told him these things, but he really listened to what you said. He started thinking there was hope, even for him. And we think that was a big step in his turning around. He discovered spiritual power and hope. He got to the place where he said, "It's the prayers of people that keeps me going."

He would write letters to people and tell them life isn't as tough as you think it is. And when you realize that a letter from David probably took him two hours to write, with six words to a page, you start to feel like a real bozo and you just don't feel sorry for yourself anymore. He is a real example of a person who on the outside has nothing going for him, but on the inside has a solid foundation and a hope. He knows where he is going, and that's most important!

*Dr. Schuller:* I think another miracle in David's life is his good humor. I used to kid him about being sure he was listening to the Hour of Power and not some other program. He came to visit me and said, "I want to show you my new tee shirt." And he opened his jacket and on his shirt were the words, "Rex Humbard, Cathedral of Tomorrow." I see he has a new tee shirt on this morning which says in green, pink and blue, "Hour of Power." You have redeemed yourself David. Tell me, Erick, what stands out most in your mind about your brother's faith?

*Erick:* I remember one thing especially. It was really a small incident, but sometimes the small things are really big things. He started having difficulty drinking through a straw, so he went to drinking right out of the glass. But then he became so weak that he couldn't even drink out of a glass. One day, he said, "Let me try to drink out of a straw." I reminded him that we knew he couldn't, but he insisted. So I went and got the straw and he could drink out of it. And as he finished drinking, he pointed to a picture of Jesus on our TV and said, "I know who's taking care of me." That was a tremendous example of how day-by-day he has to depend on God for everything. We all do, really.

David Nelson is a new friend. Virginia Chestnut is an old friend. In fact, she is a charter member of our church. When people ask me where I get my enthusiasm, I tell them that's like asking one log in a bunch of logs burning in a fireplace where it gets its flame. They all feed each other. And I've drawn my strength from the people in my congregation — people like Virginia.

*Dr. Schuller:* Tell us what happened to you, Virginia.

*Virginia:* I have Scheroderma disease. It is a circulatory disorder. Because of it I had to have one of my fingers amputated. At the time I was working as a secretary and had to learn to type without that finger. But I soon lost another finger and then realized I would lose all my fingers.

I worked for a very wonderful company. They kept me on and I became an accounting clerk so that I wouldn't have to type. But eventually the disease progressed to the point where I lost a leg. Well, I figured that I couldn't ask my boss to carry me any longer. I was divorced and had a mother and a little five-year old daughter to take care of. I prayed and I prayed that I would be healed, but I kept losing fingers. I felt God was saying, "No, I have something else in mind for you." When I lost my leg, I decided that I needed a husband, because I couldn't handle all the responsibilities. So I started to pray for one!

*Dr. Schuller:* You prayed for a man?
*Virginia:* I sure did!
*Dr. Schuller:* Yes, I think I would have joined you in that prayer.
*Virginia:* Well, God was with me all the time. With all these problems, God gave me His grace so I could face them. They weren't really problems at all, they were challenges.

Finally, one day God said, "Okay, you've weathered the storm. You've done what I've asked you to do, so here's your man." And that was when I married Bill.
*Dr. Schuller:* I remember that day ten years ago. Where do you wear your wedding band?
*Virginia:* Right here, around my neck. And with it I wear a cross—the two most important symbols in the world to me.

*Dr. Schuller:* Virginia, how do you stay so cheerful?

*Virginia:* We couldn't do it alone. The Lord lives in our lives and we just move ahead with possibility thinking!

Sometimes it is more difficult to accept chronic illness in another person than in our own body. And it is especially distressing when the other person is a child. Ken and Anita Van Wyk have worked with me for years on the church ministerial staff. Five years ago they discovered their daughter had leukemia.

*Dr. Schuller:* How did you find out?

*Anita:* We had prayed together to our Father in Heaven and thanked Him for the three healthy children He gave to us. The following morning I took Ann to the doctor because she hadn't been feeling well. After some tests, the doctor said to us, "Your daughter has acute lymphocytic leukemia."

That was a real shock. But at that time I prayed in the office, "Dear Lord, I do not know what You have in store for us in the next few years, but whatever the plan is, I know You are going to be with us every step of the way." And He really has been! Everyday has been a miracle. We still have Ann with us. We do not know what is in store for us in the future, but we know who holds the future.

*Dr. Schuller:* That's right! You received some

good news recently, didn't you, Ken?

Ken: The doctors indicated that after five years of continuous remission he would allow us to make the decision to have Ann go off her medication and have her progress checked monthly. Because we feel the Lord has His hand on her life in a very special way, we took that step and we're very grateful for what's happening.

Dr. Schuller: You know, I remember talking to the head of the Cancer Institute in New York several years ago. He said, "I think we can now say that many young people with leukemia have at least a 50% chance to live a normal life span if we catch them at the right time and if they get the right combination of medication. That was good news for both of us, I recall. What does it mean that Ann's off her medication?

Anita: Every four weeks she goes in for a bone marrow, spinal tap and blood tests. They are keeping close watch on her progression, so that in case there would be a relapse, we would catch it right away. She will do this for a year, then for the next four years we will keep close watch, only not as often.

We just want to tell you, Bob, that we have really sensed the power of people praying. There have been many times when people in the church formed a 24 hour prayer vigil for Ann. Prayer really does change things! It isn't easy to be on chemotherapy. It was hard on Ann and hard on us. There were many times when she was nauseated and had severe stomach cramps. She had cobalt therapy and for four years she did not have much hair. But whenever we'd go through an especially rough time, I'd send out an SOS to one of the prayer groups, and God would meet our needs.

*Dr. Schuller:* Ken, what stands out the most in your mind about these five years?

*Ken:* I suppose the most important word to us has been HOPE. It seemed as though the Lord kind of nudged us to release the heaviness of Ann's problem into His hands, and that liberated us to catch the brightness and warmth of hope. Our hope is anchored in a love of the Lord. We know that He loves her even more than we do, and that inspires hope within us!

*Dr. Schuller:* What would you say to someone whose situation might be similar to yours?

*Ken:* A good word would be the assurance that the Lord says to us, "I love you." It's so easy for us to feel that God has turned His back on us when something like this hits. But the Lord loves you! God will never fail you! If you relinquish your hurt, your concern, your loved one, or whatever it may be, into His masterful hand, the Lord has a way to lift you by the power of His spirit. Like a good shepherd walks with his sheep, the Lord will walk with you one step at a time, regardless of how things appear. That is hope at its highest!

Ken and Anita's daughter contracted leukemia as a young girl. Norm and Sarah Rasmussum's daughter was born Mongoloid. They had four healthy sons when they discovered they were going to have another child. They asked all their friends to pray they would have a daughter. Even the baby shower was all in pink. And when the baby was born it was a little girl. But little Leah was a Down's-Syndrome child — mongoloid. How did you feel, Norm?

*Norm:* We were crushed at that time. It was a very traumatic experience emotionally. We didn't know how to cope at first. We just knew that something had happened and the trauma was pulling us apart. You gave us a lot of encouragement during those days.

But Leah was sent by God to us and she has changed our lives completely. She's affected the lives of others as well. As she grew, she became a problem because she needed children to play with. We thought we might have to put her in an institution, but someone suggested we bring in a child from another place who needed a home. We tried that and it worked successfully. Two of the boys we brought in sixteen years ago are still living with us.

Over the years, our boys grew up and eventually moved out. And we were left with our daughter and three other children we had taken in. I had my job in the Aerospace industry and life was moving along nicely.

*Dr. Schuller:* The other three children living with you were all Down's-Syndrome children?
*Norm:* Yes. You see, like you've said so many times, we turned our problem into a project with real possibilities.
*Dr. Schuller:* What happened next?
*Sarah:* We took in a fourth child and then Norm was laid off from work. We started to think about taking in more of these children and in looking around we found a place up in Northern California that had possibilities of being enlarged. We bought this place and relocated to that area. We took the children we had with us and we enlarged our new home to where we were licensed for 34 developmentally disabled children. Since then we purchased another home where we have six children, and just within the last month we purchased another home where we are going to have six more. That makes 46 plus Leah!

*Dr. Schuller:* So your family has really grown! What are these children like? How do they come to you?
*Sarah:* They are all developmentally disabled. One of the most gratifying experiences is when one of our children, say at 14 or 15 years of age, learns to tie his or her shoes. But they also usually have some behavioral problems.

The state agencies place the children with us. Their parents are usually at the end of their ability to cope. So they come out of a real stress situation. Very often, you really can't blame either the child or the parents for the problems. It's usually a very difficult situation. So they come to a place like ours as a last hope.

*Dr. Schuller:* That must give you great satisfaction. Where do you get the strength to cope with the pressures?

*Norm:* Coming from an engineering background, I was taught that if you have a formula and you put in the right values, you will get good results. Well, over the years as we listened to you, you gave us the formula: To believe and trust in God and to always look at the possibilities. So we've been working the formula and we're just going to hang in there with it. God really can turn a mountain into a miracle!

Don't resent the unwelcomed health problems you may encounter. God can do something beautiful through them. If you've allowed resentment and bitterness to build up in your relationship with God, the place to begin is with Him.

I remember seeing a poster several years ago that said, "Jesus is the bridge over troubled waters." He is! These people have each shared how the Lord has given them hope in the face of overwhelming physical problems. He can do the same for you if you'll trust Him. Jesus is the bridge—only He can offer you HOPE!

*"But God said to me, "My grace is sufficient for you, for my power is perfected in weakness"* (2 Corinthians 12: 9 NASB).

# 5

# Conquer the Stress of Personal Failure

# Conquer the Stress
# of Personal Failure

Over the years, I have watched different people handle the stress of apparent failure after achieving varying degrees of success. Some were forced into feelings of failure either through unwelcomed retirement or through circumstances which were beyond their control. Others simply accepted failure because they were tired of the "rat-race."

Chuck Colson was one of the most powerful men in the country. He was special counsel to the President of the United States. But then he fell from power — all the way to prison. Today, he has conquered the stress of that situation because he found a purpose to live for — he loves Jesus Christ and he now ministers to prisoners all across the country.

*Chuck:* I once thought that I really knew what power was. I had all the powers that man can confer upon man: My office was next to the President's; I could fly on Air Force I; I could write executive orders on behalf of the President. But that's all pretense. It wasn't until I fell and reached the bottom that I found true fulfillment. As Christ says, I had to lose my life in order to find it. The only real power that man has ever known from the beginning of time is the power that Christ gives when He lives in our hearts.

When the Apostle Paul was writing from prison to the Christians at Philippi, he expressed what has become the life story of Chuck Colson — "I count all things to be lost." Now he was looking back on a career of success, power in life, political prominence. Before his conversion he was a member of the Sanhedran and an attorney. But he could *"count all things to be loss, in view of the surpassing value of knowing Christ Jesus my Lord, for whom I have suffered the loss of all things, and count them but rubbish in order that I may gain Christ"* (Philippians 3:8 NASB).

I suppose my life is a paradox in that all those years that I was striving to achieve power, success, wealth and prominence by the world's standards, I had to come to that one point where I realized how empty and meaningless life had become.

You know, my wife and I often sit at the breakfast table reading stacks of letters that have come in from people who watched me on the Hour of Power broadcast last year as I told the story of how I came to know Christ. Also I receive letters responding to my book, *Born Again*, the story of what God has done in my life. Patty and I weep as we read about lives being changed!

A young graduate student wrote that he was contemplating suicide until he read my book, and instead of taking his life he gave his life to Christ! Now he's working, is married, and has a lovely family. I hear from families who are reconciled, or couples broken up who through the power of Christ, come together. I have to admit that the tough, x-marine captain, the white-house hatchet man, so they called me, weeps with joy and thanksgiving to God that he changed my life and has called me to a special service.

I have been able to taste just a little of what the power of heaven is as it works in the lives of others. You know, down through the years when you see what has happened in human history, you will see that the great progress—the elimination of the slave-trade in England, that barbaric practice in the early 19th century—has not been because of what government has done, but because of God coming alive in the hearts of people!

The great Wesley awakening in England led to some of the greatest social reforms of modern times and we delude ourselves if we look to someone else to do it for us. If we think by building marble and glass temples of power in Washington that we can solve the problems of the human heart, we cannot! Because the sickness which is affecting mankind today is alienation: One person set against another, nations set against one another, races divided, families divided, divorces outpacing marriages. The answer is, *"God was in Christ and is in Christ reconciling the world to himself!"*

God has called me into the prisons and I go to them all across America. My colleagues and I find Christian inmates and invite them to live with us for two weeks in Washington, D.C. And they come to know what the beauty of fellowship is — being together with brothers and sisters who really love them. They come to know the reconciling power of love in the Lord Jesus Christ. Then they go back to prisons to finish their sentences — to live among the inmates and share with them what God has done in their lives. We have seen time and time again the paradox of God's way. God takes the fallen, the broken, the criminal and the convict and gives them the power of the risen Christ in their hearts!

We have seen magnificent things happening! Entire prison populations are having spiritual revivals! God's love is being shared in those horrible, cold, dank, dark concrete holes, known as prison, rehabilitating men where government and the prison system has failed. God does it in these prisons and we see it!

I took 12 born again inmates to the U.S. Senate to meet a U.S. Senator — many important people had shared with him but he never made a public profession of faith. These 12 men boldly witnessed to the senator and he and his wife accepted Jesus Christ! That's the way God works!

That's the unfathomable paradox of the cross of Jesus Christ — the symbol of man's greatest ignominy — to nail a criminal on the cross so no one would ever dare to follow. But instantly God converts that experience into the holiest of holy symbols. God is doing great things through the hearts of people everywhere. There is a spiritual awakening coming that is happening all across the land. It is replacing the malaise that so many have lived in and the deadness so many have experienced all around the world.

God breaks us to make us! What a joy it is. The real power is not my power, not the power of the institutions of man, but the power of Jesus Christ in our hearts! What a thrill!

You may have to fail. I pray that you do not. But I thank God for what happened to me because I found the power of the Lord Jesus

Christ. I pray that you may find the real purpose in life—the only purpose in life—the power of the risen Christ in your heart.

*Dr. Schuller:* Chuck Colson's story is told in greater detail in his book, *Born Again.* I hope you read it. But I want you to meet someone who hasn't written a book about his experience. He tasted failure, yet in his case, he was innocent. Jerald Newman is a graduate of the University of Wisconsin and lives in Greenbay, but will soon be moving to Clearwater, Florida. He was probably one of the largest and most successful land developers in the state. And then he was wrongfully accused by the newspaper of the illegal misuse of investors funds, isn't that correct?

*Jerald:* That's right. We were accused of using investor's money for personal use. I call it my personal earthquake. And as I look back I discover that each one of us is somewhat like a liberty bell in that we don't know our true values until we have our first major crack.
*Dr. Schuller:* Were the stories true?
*Jerald:* No, in fact, the next day the newspaper retracted the article word-for-word. The story contained erroneous information and was proven to be untrue. But the damage done was irreversable.
*Dr. Schuller:* The story was very damaging. What is it you called yourself?

*Jerald:* Whenever people asked what I was doing, I would tell them I had become a professional liquidator. I spent three years liquidating property as a result of the financial crisis that developed from the bad publicity. Towards the end of that time is when I accidently found the *Hour of Power* on television. When you started your message, I said to my wife, "Here's a man that I think can help me." And from that time on we have watched every program. You have given us both strength when we needed it most.

*Dr. Schuller:* Tell me how.

*Jerald:* Several ways. First, I had become quite negative during that time. Your positive message helped change my way of thinking. And you helped me think big again. Perhaps the greatest help was just to get me to be honest about myself. I found myself confessing my own weaknesses and looking to God for the answers. I got hung up on some solutions and several times did nothing but pray about it for a week or more. And all of a sudden the answers would come. That's when you know the answers are not yours, they come from God.

I've also made new commitments. I've learned to look to God in new ways. It's like salvation—you have to experience it. I've learned during this time that God not only heals bodies and heals marriages, but he rebuilds businesses. He's rebuilt mine! Today, my opportunities are over five times what they were four years ago!

*Dr. Schuller:* That's a great attitude. A purpose to live for can give you the strength to rebuild your life when it looks like all the pieces have been shattered.

But then, God has always been able to give us the strength to do the impossible. Eldridge Cleaver is a perfect example. He was once the Peace and Freedom party candidate for the President of the United States. By his own confession, he was a communist. When he went to Cuba and North Vietnam, he was treated like a king. The red carpet was rolled out. Living in exile, he enjoyed a luxurious apartment in Paris and had another place overlooking the Mediterranean Sea.

But Eldridge was running! Not just from the United States government, he was also running from himself. He was running away from the stress created by a self that had been stung and hurt by racial prejudice. He ran right into becoming a reactionary engaged in negative and violent activity. He kept on running until one day he stopped and cried out to God. Jesus Christ came into his life and turned him around. Eldridge found a *self to live with.*

*Eldridge:* There was a time when I took pride in being on the F.B.I.'s most-wanted list. But this morning I take even greater pride in being here with you, Dr. Schuller, on the Hour of Power.

Since discovering the reconciling power of Jesus Christ I have become very interested in really understanding where I missed the boat and where I went wrong. I have spent as much time as possible talking with my mother and listening to her. I've asked her a lot of questions about my past. My mother has been a real help to me in this. Recently she shared this with me: "Up until the time you were 12 years old, you were a little angel. But when you turned 12 you turned into a little devil. That's when the whole process of you going away and turning your back on the family, and dropping out of one thing or another, really began."

When I look back on that time in my life, I see a pattern of one exclusion after another. I left my family, then my circle of friends that I had grown up with. Then I quit my high school football team. Eventually, I was excluded from the normal and broad movement and got hung up in the fringe element of the Black Panther party. But ultimately, I was excluded from that part, and even from the United States itself! I found myself absolutely alone without any idea of myself, of how to get back, of how to come out of that dead-end, of how to be reunited with family and friends, and even how to come back home.

It was only after experiencing the total isolation and exclusion that I was able to be open to receiving Jesus Christ. I discovered doors

opening and a process of inclusion beginning—
the pendulum began to swing the other way! A
process of reconciliation began that could not
have possibly come about any other way! I found
myself first of all, included and reconciled with
my pursuers. The first step back was to be
reunited with the F.B.I. who was after me and
finally to come back to the country and be
reunited with family and old friends.

There's a process of healing taking place even
to the point of having the pleasure and the honor
of coming back to the Garden Grove Community
Church where I had such a wonderful experience during my first visit last year. I feel like I've
come home!

It's fantastic to see that I've gone back to
being 12 years old where I stopped listening to
my mother. I couldn't stand to hear her because
she was always trying to show me a point. But
now I just hang on to every word! It could only
happen with power—the reconciling power of
Jesus Christ!

You talk about falling from "the top?" Well,
you don't have to be a member of the White
House Staff, or a hatchet man for the president
in order to be on "the top." But you can be a
hatchet man for other causes and even a good
cause can be distorted and turned into a bad
cause because of the way you go about it! Be
careful!

I found myself on "the top" and then I found

myself at the bottom. It's great to be able to share my testimony and not put up a public facade because that is so shallow. People can see through that! It doesn't take a genius to see through a facade. I have seen through facades. I've had people pull fast ones on me and I've been able to see through it. And I know other people can see through it.

It's wonderful to be able to see how the healing power of Christ can build bridges between people, overcome generation gaps, racial tensions, stress, and class divisions. We can experience the power to break out of isolation — to overcome exclusions through Jesus Christ our Lord!

I can see myself on the road to that ultimate inclusion at the end of this earthly life when I'll be reunited with my heavenly Father! Praise God that these things are possible and that I can smile again. I have a smile inside and outside!

*Dr. Schuller:* Isn't that great! *Jesus Christ the same yesterday and today, and forever!* (Hebrews 13:8 KJV). For two thousand years that's been true. And Jesus Christ is more up to date in this scientific age than ever before. He lives to help you! He can and does.

Col. Bottomly was running, only he ran the way you're supposed to. He didn't have any problems with the law. In fact, he was on his way to the top — a general in the Air Force. But he calls himself a prodigal father. What in the world is a prodigal father?

*Col. Bottomly:* My life study is how an American boy can, by the way he is born and raised and trained, become a fighter. It may not be in the streets or in the military service. It could just as easily be in industry or commerce. But while he is growing up he is molded into becoming a fighter-type of person.

*Dr. Schuller:* Are you that kind of person?

*Col. Bottomly:* Yes, I'm a perfect example. I'm also an example of how a person by self-reliance, discipline and life-style, can separate himself from God. I thought I could do it all by myself. I didn't need any help — not even from God. The longer a person thinks like that and the more he succeeds, the more he believes that. But God can still break into any man's heart, and my book, *Prodigal Father*, tells how God got into my heart.

*Dr. Schuller:* How did God get into your life?

*Col. Bottomly:* As a wing commander in Southeast Asia, I rose to a real crest of power, glory and pride. One day I was so proud, so glorious and so filled with a sense of power that I felt I could violate the rules of war. I bombed across the border in North Vietnam, even though I knew I was not allowed to do so. I violated the discipline of the air, which every pilot knows he cannot do. I was called on the carpet and faced a court martial for violating the President's *orders.*

In that terrible situation, where my whole career was threatened, I remembered that my son had become a Christian while at the Air Force Academy. He had asked me several times to allow him to share with me the joy and beauty and power of his Christian life, but I had never taken the time to listen.

But those few days I was grounded and waiting to hear about my court martial were times filled with tremendous stress, trial and tribulation. I was desperate! Finally, I called my son long distance all the way from Thailand. He shared with me the joy of being a child of God. I prayed with him over the phone and received Jesus Christ as my Savior. And miracles began to happen!

*Dr. Schuller:* What happened about the court martial?

*Col. Bottomly:* That was one of the miracles. It didn't happen, but I did lose my command and the chance to be promoted to General.

*Dr. Schuller:* And you consider yourself to be a baby in the faith. Well, you're a tough looking baby! I think it's great, that just because you're a Christian doesn't mean you cease to be tough. Christians are tough, but they're tender inside. Tell me, how has life changed for you since you've become a Christian?

*Col. Bottomly:* I think my attitudes and my

outlook have changed the most. Of course, our family has really changed also. Within a year-and-a-half my wife and each of my five children had become Christians. We weren't really a family before. We were scattered nomads not only spiritually but physically as well. My older children were scattered across the country living with friends and relatives, drifting through life without any real meaning and purpose. Jesus Christ pulled our family together into the closest, most devoted, loving family you could imagine.

*Dr. Schuller:* That's tremendous! Let me say something very personal. You twinkle; your eyes really do. It's great to see that in a tough Colonel with 33 years of military service behind him.

Personal failure can be conquered when you have a *purpose to live for*, a *self to live with*, and a *faith to live by*. Corrie Ten Boom had everything going for her in Holland. She had a loving family and a successful trade. But then Hitler moved in and started killing the Jews. As faithful Christians, the Ten Boom family did everything they could to save their Jewish friends. She and her family risked their lives daily!

Then one morning, Gestapo agents stormed into their home and demanded to know where the Jews were hidden. Corrie, her sister Betsie, and her father were caught and forcibly taken from their home. Her father was sent to one concentration camp, Corrie and her sister to another one. Both her father and her sister died while in prison. Only a miracle allowed Corrie to be released. She knows stress as few people have known stress. She conquered stress because she has a *faith to live by!*

*Corrie:* I'm glad that I can tell you a little about that faith. I have several chapters of my life that I'd like to share with you.

First, I was in a happy home with Father and Betsie, my sister. I had a good watchmaking business and I was the first licensed woman watchmaker. Then came that terrible time when I had to be in prison. Following that I had a chapter in which I was a tramp for the Lord — 33 years! And now I am in a new chapter. I am now an alien resident of America. I am happy for that because now I am no longer a tramp! The Lord has given me a house where I work on the book I am writing.

Oh, you might think I'm retiring. Not at all. You call it retirement, I just say I have new tires!

A faith to live by — what is that faith? The Bible tells us very clearly: Faith in Jesus Christ! 1 John 5:5 says: *In fact this faith of ours is the only way in which the world has been conquered.* "For who could ever be said to conquer the world, in the true sense, except the ones who really believe that Jesus is God's son?'' (paraphrased)

I came to know Jesus when I was five years old. He has been with me since then and has never let me down. And I can tell you what it means when you have to go through life and have a difficult stress-filled time.

When I was in prison I learned more than ever what it means to know about the cross of Jesus Christ. Two thousand years ago he died for the sins of the world—for my sins! The Bible says, *"Who is he that overcomes the world? He that believes Jesus is the Son of God"* (I John 5:5 KJV) I learned that when you have Jesus Christ, you possess divine power that can silence the enemy and inflict upon him the danger he would inflict upon you! That is faith in Jesus Christ.

He makes us more than conquerors! Yes, He is the victory that overcomes the world! And He gives you, not a spirit of fear, but the spirit of power and of love and of a sound mind. The greatest joy I've known was in that terrible prison camp where 95,000 women were either killed or died—my sister included. I discovered there that when you have Jesus Christ, He not only influences your life now. He gives you the great promise of the future!

Paul wrote in Romans 8, *In my opinion, whatever you have to go through now, is less than nothing compared to the magnificent future God has planned for us.* The best is yet to come! And when we have received Jesus Christ as our Savior our life here is victorious. The great thing is that we will see Him face-to-face and we will see the embroidery of our lives from his side. And we will then be able to praise and thank the Lord like never before in this life!

People say that I have a great faith. Perhaps some of you say your faith is not so great, but the Bible tells us not to look at our faith, but to look at Jesus who is the author and finisher of our faith! And when you look at Him, you see that He can make you victorious. It doesn't matter if our faith is small. If there's only faith in that great God and great Savior Jesus Christ, then we know the truth that Jesus said, *If your faith is as small as a mustard seed, it is sufficient to remove mountains.* So let us look to Jesus!

Look around and be depressed.
Look to Jesus and be addressed!

You have to accept Jesus Christ as your Savior today! Remain in the boundaries where God's love can reach and comfort you. Say "yes" to Jesus and you will be coming to the one who said, *"Come unto me and I will give you rest!"* "Come all!" He says. And that means you! He'll share with you what it means to know Him personally. And then you'll experience a *faith you can live by!*

*Dr. Schuller:* You too can find this faith!  You

can move mountains of stress as you place your life in God's hands.

George Foreman discovered faith in the most unlikely situation. He's been a favorite of the fans, ever since his victories in the Mexico Olympics. His career as a professional led to the heavyweight title of Champion of the World.

*Dr. Schuller:* George, you look different today than you did when you were with us several months ago. You have a different distinct glow on your face.

*George:* Maybe it's because I'm the happiest I have ever been in my whole life.

*Dr. Schuller:* You lost the fight with Jimmy Young and you're the happiest you've ever been?

*George:* Right. And it was that fight that brought it about. For the first time I experienced death—death in my own life. And it frightened me so much. I was in the dressing room with my trainers and my doctor. They all thought that I was tired. But every thought I had led me to think more and more about death. I didn't know what was happening. I started thinking of all kinds of ways to avoid these overpowering thoughts. I wanted to walk or take a shower. But then all of a sudden I was completely overtaken by the feeling I was going to die.

*Dr. Schuller:* But you didn't get knocked out in the ring, did you?

*George:* I didn't even have a hard fight. I wasn't hurting any place either, but a great fear overtook me that I was going to die. I started saying to myself, "I believe in God. Why am I afraid to die. I've prepared myself." But I was so frightened.

*Dr. Schuller:* How did Jesus Christ get into the picture?

*George:* For some reason I started talking to Him. I started making bargains. I told God I could still make contributions. I could go around witnessing. But He said He didn't want my contributions and He didn't want me to go on talking. He wanted me! All this time I was trying to tell my trainer and my doctor what was happening, but they didn't understand. When Jesus came into my life in the locker room I jumped up and started running around the room yelling, "Hallelujah, I've been born again!" I mean I shouted it. I wanted everyone to know that God had changed my life. That's when my doctor sent me to the hospital and they took all kinds of examinations to see if I had been hurt or something. They thought I'd gone crazy.

*Dr. Schuller:* You look pretty healthy to me.

*George:* They couldn't find anything wrong with me. I am healthy and happy. You know, I've been the heavyweight champion of the world, I won the Olympic gold medals and I've gone to the bank with a check for five million dollars. But I've never really been happy. But I'm happy now! I'm glad I lost that fight because it was the greatest victory I've ever had. People were praying for me and now I've got something money or fame can't buy. I'm a whole man now!

*Dr. Schuller:* You called me soon after you got out of the hospital. Why did you call?

*George:* I wanted to share my experience with you and see if you thought I was crazy. I know I'm not crazy because I've got so many assurances from the Bible. I've never looked at the Bible, but I read it all the time now. I'm just like a vacuum cleaner. I just suck it all in. I don't want you to call me champ. I want God to be champ now. I just thank God for what's happened to me!

God never lets anything happen to you unless it is loaded with opportunities. You may not be facing a prison sentence or have lost your family in a concentration camp. But there is a point in your life that hurts. It may be a failure within your family. You may feel like tossing in the towel at your place of employment. You may think there is no hope for your situation. I want you to know that when you go through the valley of trouble, God can turn it into a spring of new life! When you know Jesus Christ as your Savior, you can conquer the stress of personal failure. Open your life to Him so that . . .

*. . . you will be filled with his mighty, glorious strength so that you can keep going no matter what happens—always full of the joy of the Lord* (Colossians 1:11 TLB).

# 6

# Conquer the
# Stress of
# Impossible Tasks

# Conquer the
# Stress of
# Impossible Tasks

Do you want to conquer stress? Then be prepared for some problems, for every solution brings with it its own particular and peculiar set of difficulties. It is the so-called impossibilities of life that create the greatest opportunities. Problems are really the challenges to keep us young and alive. The adventurous person boldly faces the impossible, know that with God, all things are possible.

Steve Van Meter is one of these people. He's a young man who thrives on the adventure of climbing mountains. Steve, when did you start climbing real mountains?

*Steve:* About three or four years ago. That's when I became seriously interested. Soon after that I climbed Mt. McKinley.

*Dr. Schuller:* That's in Alaska, isn't it? That

mountain's 20,000 feet high! Did you walk up or did you use ropes?

*Steve:* Well, the particular route we used was the snowshoe type about half way up. But then it became technical from there on and we had to use ropes. We took the easiest route, but this summer I'm going back to do the difficult south-face which requires several thousand feet of rope.

*Dr. Schuller:* Have you done any climbing in Yosemite?

*Steve:* I was climbing on El Capitan about a month ago, but we had a snow storm knock us off and we had to come down.

*Dr. Schuller:* Why do you subject yourself to the stress of climbing?

*Steve:* I don't really have an answer to that. It is challenging and there is a certain romance involved. But at the same time, when I get out there on a slope, or an ice wall, or in the crevasses, I often wonder what on earth I'm doing there. I could be back home enjoying myself. But there is always a sense of pride when you reach your goal and get back.

*Dr. Schuller:* Aren't you planning to lead an expedition scheduled for a major climb next year?

*Steve:* Yes, we have a six man team that will attempt to climb Annapurna. This mountain is just under 25,000 feet and is about 150 miles west of Mt. Everest in the Himalayas. We have a cinematographer coming with us who will film the entire climb.

Only two other groups have climbed the mountain. A Japanese women's team in 1972 and an Indian team before that. This will be the first American attempt and we'll be climbing an unclimbed route. We'll have some pretty dangerous icefalls to go through at the bottom.

*Dr. Schuller:* What are the dangers involved in a climb like this?
*Steve:* There are quite a few: crevasses, avalanches, rock falls and the effects of the altitude without oxygen. We won't be using any oxygen on our climb.

I had a close call, once, while climbing Mt. McKinley. I fell into a crevasse, which was about a half-mile long. But the place I fell was the only spot that was narrow enough to hold me. I went out of my tent to take some photographs of the glacier we were on. It was supposed to be solid ice, but there was a huge crack, or crevasse right near us. And there was a snow pack over it so you couldn't see the crevasse. All of a sudden I went down, but because this was the narrow spot, I only went down to my arm pits. But my feet were dangling over a hole that was at least 200 feet below.

But that marked a turning point in my life. While I was dangling there, I decided I had better do something about my faith. After searching for over two years, I invited Jesus Christ into my life.

*Dr. Schuller:* Steve, you're a new Christian, but living the Christian life is not too different from climbing mountains. The pathway looks so solid, but there are crevasses underneath. You told me earlier that ever since that time, you never travel on a glacier without being roped to someone else. It's great, as a Christian, to be roped to Jesus Christ. I congratulate you for your courage and for your faith.

Sometimes the tasks we face are completely beyond our control. I'm thinking of the demands we place upon ourselves to live up to the expectations of a parent or to compete with a successful older brother or sister. Bill Bailey knows that kind of stress. Bill, can I ask you a personal question? Your brother, F. Lee Bailey is very famous. In some ways you must feel like you're living under his shadow. How do you handle that?

*Bill:* That has created problems, especially since we are partners in law. But I suppose being the younger relative of any famous person creates problems. Dr. Schuller, your sermon on "How to Handle Your Competition Creatively," has been a real help to me. I read that and said to myself, "If I'm trying to compete with Lee, there's no way I'll ever win because there is only one F. Lee Bailey. But there's only one Bill

Bailey, so I'd better work on being the best Bill Bailey around!"

*Dr. Schuller:* Seeing that you're a graduate of Harvard University and the Harvard Law School, I feel honored.

*Bill:* It's an honor for Rene and me to be with you. I was standing in the lobby before the service and someone came up to me and asked, "Are you from this area?" I said, "No, I'm from Boston." And they looked at me and remarked, "That's quite a ways to go to attend church, isn't it?" But being here fulfills a dream that Rene and I have had for about a year now.

*Dr. Schuller:* What is that?

*Bill:* After I graduated from Harvard, I went into the practice of law for a few years. Then I joined with a client who was in the real estate business and I got completely wrapped up in development, investing and so forth. Both of us became millionaires. I was very proud of all that, but then suddenly hard times came and things started falling apart. Not just financially, but my whole spirit fell apart.

Sometimes on Sunday mornings I would let Rene sleep late and I would go into my den looking at a piece of paper with a list of all the problems for the week. Kind of like wallowing in my problems. But one Sunday I turned on the TV and didn't feel like watching the cartoons. As I flipped the dial I saw an attractive man standing there talking about positive thinking and possibilities. I thought to myself that this was great for other people, but it just didn't fit me. But week after week I sat there and watched and listened. I read your materials and listened to your tapes. And following your sermon on "Alter your Altars" I realized that in the process of building a real estate empire I was building for myself and not for God. That was my mistake. So I made up my mind then to start over again and to make God my partner in whatever I did thereafter.

*Dr. Schuller:* Bill, you told me something last night about what you did at the end of that program.

*Bill:* You said that wherever a person was, they could kneel down and ask Christ to come into their heart. And I did. There are times while growing up when you see public displays of religion that you sense is the result of people wearing religion on their sleeves. But then there are times when you know this is what you need to do to show the reality of your faith from within. So I got down on my knees and I prayed out loud right along with you on TV. And this past year has been great as God has been helping me become the best Bill Bailey around!

*Dr. Schuller:* Thanks Bill, God loves you and so do I.

You've probably never heard of Linda and Rock Bradford, but the impossible tasks they have faced and conquered are familiar to many. Today they are beautiful Christian people. Tell me how you've become such a glowing couple.

*Linda:* To begin with, for the first thirteen years of our marriage we really didn't have Jesus Christ in our lives. We were looking for happiness in all the wrong places. We thought we could buy it or something on that order. But we never could find relief from the stress, or peace of mind either. But we kept on searching. Finally, Rock was in St. Joseph's Hospital . . .

*Rock:* . . . And in the room with me was Frank Boss. That was some time ago, but I can still remember the excitement he created in that room!

*Dr. Schuller:* Frank was the treasurer of the Hour of Power and the superintendent of the construction of the Tower of Hope. That was his first cancer operation, wasn't it?

*Rock:* Right. Both Linda and I saw the joy in his life and we just couldn't believe it. But I was discharged from the hospital and we got back into our parties and soon forgot Frank and his joy.

*Linda:* But it was a seed planted in our lives. I started watching the Hour of Power and felt your messages spoke directly to a need in my life. So my daughters and I started coming to church. Rock stopped drinking long enough to come on Christmas Eve.

*Rock:* When I arrived, Dr. Schuller, you were

standing in the back. I walked up to you and your hand was outstretched. I think that was when we became 50/50 Christians. We were on the right track.

*Linda:* The real turn-around came as a result of a little baby we had and lost. Last year I was blessed with a pregnancy after nine years. We felt we were really getting our lives together at that point. We were coming to church regularly and were filled with the love and joy of Christ. On the night following Easter, I went into labor and had a beautiful boy. Our two daughters are 13 and 9 and we all felt a miracle had come into our lives with this little boy. Boys are not common in our families, and we had trouble choosing a name. We were so overwhelmed, we actually left the hospital with the baby unnamed.

The morning after we brought him home, we got a call from the hospital asking for his name. We had decided on Michael David and they noted their records. About an hour later, our new little boy left us to return to heaven.

I remember during my seventh month of pregnancy, we were sitting here in church and you were talking about babies. In your sermon you said that when babies are born, the doctor always tells the mother whether it is a boy or a girl. But the parents never ask "Does my baby have wings?" They only check his fingers and toes. So we put on Michael David's headstone, "He never lost his wings." This is because we really felt that he was a miracle and had been sent to us for a reason. So many beautiful and wonderful things have resulted.

*Rock:* Our lives have changed as a result. In fact, the night before the funeral we came to the Candlelight Service and completely rededicated our lives to Jesus Christ. From that time on it has been marvelous.We have found that inner peace we had been searching for.

*Dr. Schuller:* Linda, some women might be saying right now, "My husband will never change!" What would you say to them?

*Linda:* Well, Rock was an alcoholic. I used to pray that God would help him to stop drinking and that he would start going to church. And I just talked to the Lord about it. Because He's the only one that can work that kind of miracle.

*Rock:* It took some time, but slowly God got through to me. Now I'm so excited about life that I just want more and more of God. I own my own business, and business is just fantastic with this new outlook. Instead of not wanting to get up in the morning, I just can't wait. I get up early because I'm so excited for the new day.

*Dr. Schuller:* When you have Jesus Christ in your life, every day is more exciting than the previous day. It's just a beautiful life!

I met Anne's husband, Benno, a number of

years ago. I was still in the drive-in church and God gave me a dream of a church that could be both a walk-in and drive-in at the same time. I went to Richard Neutra's architectural firm, and there I met Benno Fischer. As we talked, I noted a "K" and an "L" tattooed on his hand and I asked him what it stood for. He told me it was the initials for the German words for Concentration Camp. Benno is one of ten children and he was the only one to survive the Nazi holocaust. His wife, Anne, was one of eight children and she was the only one in her family to survive. Anne, tell us about yourself.

*Anne:* Well, I am a Jew and I am a survivor of the Nazi horrors. So naturally, my story is not really a very happy one. It's the story of man's inhumanity to man.

As we know, from the ashes of the six million Jews who perished in the extermination camps and concentration camps, a new Jewish State was reborn in the land of Israel. And for my own life and for the life of my husband, through a set of really miraculous circumstances we have each been given a new life.

*Dr. Schuller:* How did it begin?

*Anne:* When Poland was invaded by the Nazi Germans in September 1939, the Nazis declared that being born a Jew was an unforgivable crime, punishable only by death. The tortuous road of suffering, persecution, moral and physical pain, hunger and death had begun.

First, we were all herded into ghettos. All our human and civil rights were taken away from us. We were piled together with three or four families sharing one room. Then the Nazis started what they called the final solution. We were jammed into cattle trains, 100 or more people to one car, and shipped to the camps. One day I found myself on one of those trains.

*Dr. Schuller:* How old were you then, Anne?

*Anne:* By then I was 21 years old. I was 18 when the war started and had just finished high school. My father had already been killed, and so had two of my brothers. As we were jammed into the cattle cars, we were separated from whatever family we had left. I was alone. The conditions were absolutely unbearable. There was groaning, crying and suffocation. And there were Germans shooting at us through those little openings in the cattle cars.

The train was traveling about 40 miles per hour and it was getting dark. I suppose we traveled at night so as not to attract the attention of the villagers. Suddenly, some desperate young man who was near one of the larger openings simply started picking up people and pushing them out of the car into the night. I was one of those shoved out of the train. I heard some shots ring out behind me as I flew through the air. I didn't quite know what was happening, but suddenly I found myself lying in a ditch.

*Dr. Schuller:* Were you hurt?

*Anne:* I lay there for some time, not quite conscious of what was going on. When I regained my senses I started touching myself. I discovered that I was in one piece and had not broken any bones. I didn't quite know where to go or what to do, but I picked myself up and started to walk. It took me sixteen days to walk back to the town I was taken from. During this time I slept in the woods. Sometimes I would knock at the door of a peasant hut, and if they were not terribly afraid of my appearance or the thought that I was probably a Jew, they would give me a bit of bread.Others would simply chase me away.

Sometimes at night I would steal into a barn, hide under the hay and get a few hours of sleep. Once, during a heavy downpour, I saw an open brick factory with a little roof over one part. I walked in and fell asleep. I must have been asleep for a couple of hours when suddenly someone touched me on my shoulder. I woke up and saw a young boy with his cows. He asked, "What are you doing here?" I told him I had come in out of the rain and had fallen asleep. "Are you hungry?" he asked. And when I answered yes, he shared one of the two cakes his mother had probably given him for his lunch. His love helped me keep going.

When I finally made my way back to my town, I was all alone and didn't know what to do. There were very, very few Jews left there and they had mostly given up any hope. Somebody put the idea in my mind to apply to the German employment office. We knew they were sending able-bodied young men and women to Germany to do their poorest labor, because most of the German labor force was on the front.

By the providence of God, I had blonde hair and blue eyes, so they didn't recognize me as a Jew. I was given a train ticket and went to Germany, where I worked in a hospital as a Polish, non-Jewish, alien slave laborer for almost three years. I worked there until the war ended. My liberation day was Friday the thirteenth of April, 1945. Needless to say I consider Friday the thirteenth to be a very lucky day for me.

*Dr. Schuller:* So the war was over and you were still alive. Your whole family had perished and you were alone in Stuttgart. Before the war, you were in love with a young man named Benno Fischer.

*Anne:* Yes, we had met in 1940. But as far as I knew, he had died. But the very next day I was standing, waiting for a bus in Stuttgart when I noticed a young man walking back and forth behind me. He was kind of giving me the eye. Suddenly, I realized it was Benno and turned and said, "Benno, you are alive!" It was another miracle and the beginning of our life together. One thing we learned during those dark days was to keep our sense of humor. A Jewish

humorist once said, "The very important thing
in life is to keep on laughing. And even if there is
nothing to laugh about, laugh on credit."
*Dr. Schuller:* And I am certain you have a deep
appreciation for life and all its blessings.

What impossible tasks do you face? Perhaps it
doesn't seem as difficult as surviving the Nazi
concentration camps or winning over alcoholism.
But the tasks you face are the most important
ones simply because you are the one facing
them. You can be strong in the face of
overwhelming odds. The beautiful possibilities
that lie hidden in every seemingly impossible
task are waiting to be discovered by the person
who is willing to trust in God and His wisdom. I
want to personally encourage you with the words
of St. Paul:

> *Finally, be strong in the Lord, and in
> the power of His might!* (Ephesians
> 6:10 KJV).

# 7

# Conquer
# Inner Stress

# Conquer Inner Stress

Sometimes we feel under stress because of the mountainous tasks that loom in our future. But there are some people who face stress simply because of the demands they place upon themselves. I call this inner stress.

Inner stress can result from a tendency to be a perfectionist. It can also develop as we push ourselves to become the best possible person we can be. The quest for excellence can produce stress that wears us out or strengthens us for the journey.

Tom Netherton is a familiar face to millions of us. Every week he is one of the featured soloists on the Lawrence Welk Show. Tom, you have a wonderful Christian mother, don't you? I know, because I received a letter from her telling me about you.

*Tom:* I praise the Lord for a mom like her.She's been a continual help to me.

*Dr. Schuller:* She told me about the vital personal faith you have. Tell us how you found this faith.

*Tom:* I came to know Jesus Christ when I was in the armed services. I was in the Army stationed in Panama. But it took a long time for the Lord to get through to me. For three years He pounded away at my brain. I met Christians who talked about Jesus in a personal way. They talked about a personal Lord they could talk to on a one-to-one basis. I had never known that. At first I thought they were strange, and yet at the same time I saw something very real in their lives. I finally reached a point where I couldn't reject what I was seeing.

So, one day at a revival meeting in a Baptist church in Panama, I gave my life to Jesus Christ. The preacher said it was only because of Jesus Christ physically living inside of us that we Christians were whole and complete. And that was the key that opened up my understanding. I wanted to be the kind of man that God wanted me to be and I saw that I couldn't do it without the presence and power of the Lord.

Ever since then, it has been a tremendous life. I say "tremendous" carefully, because it has not always been a bed of roses. But always, God is dealing with me and working with me. No one really likes to admit who we really are and what we are really like. But God brings the real you to the surface. He deals with you personally and takes away all the guilt. I praise God for His wonderful love towards me.

*Dr. Schuller:* Tom, when you made a commitment to Jesus Christ, what happened? Did bells ring or did you see big flashes of light?

*Tom:* No, not really. The Bible says, "The Holy Spirit witnesses to us that we are Sons of God." I said, "Lord, forgive me for my sins and I trust you to take away my sins and my guilt. I recognize that it is by your shed blood that this can be possible. I thank you for it." And when I sincerely prayed that prayer, I just knew that God did what He said He would do. There was a feeling, yes, but it wasn't a gigantic sensation. I guess it was just that I finally felt whole!

*Dr. Schuller:* You felt you had arrived at what you were meant to be. That's marvelous. How did you happen to land this exciting spot with Lawrence Welk every week?

*Tom:* Again, I praise the Lord because He worked all of that out. I started to Bible College, but felt the Lord wanted me to leave and go into entertainment. When things didn't work out, I just figured that maybe I had misunderstood and that God really didn't want me in that work. So I decided to go into gospel singing. But that didn't work out either. Out of frustration, I took a summer job singing in an outdoor musical pageant in Madora, North Dakota. That's about

120 miles west of Bismark. Harold and Sheila Shaffer owned the show and as I got to know them, they responded to what the Lord was doing in my life, and they called Lawrence Welk to set up an audition. I met Lawrence and you know the rest of the story.

*Dr. Schuller:* Tom, what would you say to people today facing stress?

*Tom:* One thing—life isn't worth living without Jesus Christ. You'll be frustrated all your life until you give in completely to the Lord. Only when you do that do you finally know what it means to be a full, total person and enjoy fellowship with God and with your fellow man.

*Dr. Schuller:* I'll second that! Thanks Tom.

If you are a Walt Disney film fan, then the face of Dean Jones is very familiar. His career has been successful for a number of years, but he recently had an experience that helped him discover a new source of strength in his life.

*Dean:* About two years ago I started rehearsals for a new film. Suddenly it hit me that I was caught in a pattern that I had been rehearsing for fifteen years. I was working at glorifying Dean Jones! I wanted standing ovations, good reviews, and all the other remaining glories that are inherent in my business. But I realized that none of these things had satisfied the deep spiritual need of my life. If I kept on getting good reviews and standing ovations for another fifteen years, I still wouldn't be satsified. Three days later, I had an awareness of God where His presence was so real to me that it was almost a physical thing. I could feel Him present with me and I praise God for that experience!

*Dr. Schuller:* And that's when you accepted Christ into your life?

*Dean:* Yes. Shortly after that experience, my wife and I dedicated our lives to Jesus Christ, and we're following Him as close as we know how.

You know, the Lord wanted me to talk about victory today. I used to think victory was an old-fashioned word. When I was a kid, I used to hear my father say, "You've got to get the victory, son," but I never knew what he meant. I never before knew what it was like to have spiritual victory in my life. We're not supposed to be victims of the world, we're supposed to be victors through Jesus Christ.

*Dr. Schuller:* Wasn't your commitment tested soon after that?

*Dean:* I made a rather boastful statement one night to a couple visiting in our home. I said, "You know, in light of my new commitment to the Lord, I could give up my career and even my money. Even this house," I continued, "I love this house and we've been so happy here. But if it burned down tomorrow, I could still praise the Lord!"

And the next morning at 11:00, the house was

in flames. We don't know how it started, but a third of the house was destroyed, along with some good motorcycles and a car. I said to my wife, Laurie, "We have to praise the Lord for this fire!"

I know that sounds illogical and crazy, but I believe you praise God even for your difficulties! And by praising Him, you will have spiritual victory. If you have victory in the spirit, it's not long before that victory will be seen in the rest of your life.

*Dr. Schuller:* That's good possibility thinking! God packages great possibilities in the most difficult problems! This is fantastic. Dean, you've found that your commitment to Christ has made the difference in all of your relationships.

*Dean:* Absolutely! And if Christ can help me in the theater, where we face unbelievable stresses, then Jesus Christ can give victory in every walk of life and in your home!

*Dr. Schuller:* Dean, there's a sparkle in your eyes. Your victory shows!

You may recognize Dean Jones' face, but every American will recognize Thurl Ravenscroft's voice. Thurl, how are you today?

*Thurl:* Dr. Schuller, now that I've met you and now that I'm on the *Hour of Power*, and now that I have Jesus Christ in my life—in the words of Tony the Tiger, I feel Grrrrrrreat!

*Dr. Schuller:* Almost makes me want a bowl of cereal! How long have you been a Christian, Thurl?

*Thurl:* I became a Christian forty years ago on another radio ministry. I was the bass in a quartet and we sang for Josea Hopkins and the Little Country Church of Hollywood. That's where I became a Christian.

Shortly after that, I had an opportunity to leave the Country Church and go into show business. It was quite a struggle, but the Lord said, "I need Christians in show business as much as I need them in gospel work." And I'm proof of the fact that once you accept Jesus, He never leaves you. He's been by my side ever since, even in show business.

*Dr. Schuller:* What are some of the things you've done in show business, besides Tony the Tiger? Haven't you done a lot of the voices in the Disney films?

*Thurl:* Yes, I've been fortunate to do a lot of voices in the Disney productions and at Disneyland. In the pirates of the Caribbean, you can hear my voice all over. In Bear Country Jamboree, I'm the voice of Buff, on the wall. And in the Enchanted Tiki Room, I'm the God of Life—Thunderoa. Plus I do other things around the park. In fact, if you're really quick, you can see me in the Haunted Mansion. They have a bust of me there.

*Dr. Schuller:* Thurl, you've faced a lot of stress,

I'm sure, over the years in show business. I really believe God can intervene in a human life and perform beautiful miracles. Do you believe that?

*Thurl:* Yes, indeed. I recall about eleven years ago, I was under some real pressure in my work when suddenly I was faced with a very serious physical problem. Through prayer, and the laying on of hands, I was healed. I went into surgery, but there was nothing for the surgeon to do. God had already done everything. So I know the power of Jesus Christ. In fact, I have written a dramatic reading that shows the life-changing power of our Savior.

I am sure that it is a scene that you are all familiar with. Here Jesus is on the cross, crucified between two thieves. One turns to Him and says, "If you are who you say you are, why don't you save yourself and save us, too?" The other turns and says, "Be quiet! Don't you know this man has done nothing wrong and we are getting what we deserve."

I would like you to imagine with me now, that it is shortly after the crucifixion. And as I stand before you I am that penitent thief and you are able to hear what is deep within my heart and soul. It might sound something like this.

"A thief knows a thief. A thief can smell an

honest man a mile away. How else do you think we know enough not to rob our own kind, eh?

"The first time I saw this man I knew he was not my kind. He had no curse for the man who drove the spikes, no damnation for those who spit at him and taunted him.

"And then in that moment when His cross was raised next to mine, I knew who he was and my heart was filled with pity. I remember I had seen him once before standing by the lake laughing with friends while children played around his feet. My fellow thief and I were passing by looking for a place to come back to at night and rob. And my pal said, 'You see that guy over there. He claims to be the Messiah.' So we stopped to hear him speak.

"We saw a blind man given back his sight; half a hundred sick people made well and went on their way. My pal left me that day an honest man heading for the Temple to do penance. But me, I was young and a fool and I closed my heart and stumbled blindly on my way.

"Then today, I met Jesus again, and I couldn't help but wonder if I had a second chance. I turned to Him and said, 'Jesus, remember me when you come into your kingdom.' At his answer, my heart burst within me, for he said, 'Today you'll be with me in paradise.'

"Now I know man is never more than a breath away from dying. But now I know that man is never more than a breath away from living with God!"

*Dr. Schuller:* Thurl has discovered the source of strength—Jesus Christ. Another person who has successfully tapped that source of strength and conquered inner stress is Rhonda Fleming. Rhonda, what has God done in your life?

*Rhonda:* I hardly know where to begin! Well, I'm going to share this with you. I've never told this story before, but I love your ministry and I love the people connected with the *Hour of Power*. That special hour has meant so much to me when I've been out on the road in a lonely hotel room. And as many performers have said, your ministry, Dr. Schuller, has been a precious friend that has lifted me to the skies and helped me to feel God's presence through that television screen.

When I was eighteen years old, I was a very lost little girl. This happens to many teenagers for some reason. I felt unloved even though I had a wonderful mother who had regularly taken me to church through the years. I'd heard about God but He didn't really mean all that much to me. I thought I didn't need Him. But late one night—I think it was about 1:00 in the morning—I drove to a knoll of the hill and sat in my little car. I prayed, "If there is a God, then speak to me now and help me because I'm very lonely and very lost. I just don't know where I'm going."

It was very cold that night and my teeth were chattering. I don't know if I cried or not, but I was very demanding. I demanded an answer from God, if he existed.

I don't know how long I was there, but suddenly a presence came into that little car and touched the top of my head as firmly as if you did it right now. God, the Holy Spirit, was there with a very definite touch. Where moments before I was cold, there went through me such a warmth that I felt I was on fire. I could feel heat pulsating through my blood and my body. And then the love exploded and just poured in. I couldn't wait to start the engine of that little jalopy and race home.

*Dr. Schuller:* You were warmed by the love of Christ!

*Rhonda:* Yes! It was God giving me a direct answer to the deep need for love and assurance that I was crying out for at that moment. I'll *never* forget that experience!

*Dr. Schuller:* Was that experience before you went into show business?
*Rhonda:* Yes. My career in the motion picture industry started soon after that. But I quickly took over the reins of my life instead of remembering that I had to allow God to continue to be number one in my life. I had to learn that the hard way. I had to be brought to my knees. I

thank God that He understood me so well.

*Dr. Schuller:* Did you ever tire of your career? I imagine there is a lot of inner stress in that profession as you drive yourself to perfection. Did you ever long for a simple life?

*Rhonda:* About five years ago, I thought it would be the greatest thing in the world to quit working. I could just stay home, read good books, travel, and become what I thought would be a normal woman. I did that for five years, only to discover that one of the greatest gifts in the world is working. And I also discovered that God can only use us when we are active.

During those five years I became emotionally, spiritually and creatively stagnant. I was lost. I thought I was going to die on the vine. Suddenly I realized that I had shut myself off from the mainstream of life. People were wondering if Rhonda Fleming was still alive.

I am so grateful for the opportunity to be working again. I told God, "I've messed up my life. Please take it over and help to fix the mess I've created." And He did. That's when the opportunities came and the doors opened again. I went to New York and did my first Broadway show!

*Dr. Schuller:* You told me earlier that someone sent you a copy of the Possibility Thinkers Creed.

*Rhonda:* It arrived at just the right time. I kept two of them with me in New York—one in my stage dressing room and one in my hotel room. God used that to give me strength. I know it by heart:

When faced with a mountain, I WILL NOT QUIT!
I will keep on striving until I climb over, find a pass through, tunnel underneath—or simply stay and turn the mountain into a gold mine, WITH GOD'S HELP!

And it's true. God has really helped me!
*Dr. Schuller:* God bless you, Rhonda. God loves you and so do I.

Not everyone faces the kind of stress actors, actresses, and other artists encounter. As they strive for excellence, they push themselves to the limit. And this creates inner stress.

But each of us sets personal goals which we hope to achieve. And in the process, we push ourselves to perform to the best of our ability. Jesus said, "With God, all things are possible!" When you start to live these powerful words, you push yourself to do things other people consider impossible. But the impossible only becomes possible with God! If you are trying to do it alone, you will not make it. Invite the power-source into your life. Let Jesus Christ turn your stress into strength!

*But they that wait upon the Lord shall renew their strength. They shall mount up with wings like eagles; they shall run and not be weary; they shall walk and not faint.* (Isaiah 40:31 TLB).

# 8

# Conquer
# Situational Stress

# Conquer
# Situational Stress

Some stress is caused by our efforts to achieve our objectives. Some stress may result from things that happen to us. But there is another kind of stress which occurs when it looks like the whole world around us is falling apart. I call this situational stress. What can you do if your situation — your location in life — is causing stress? Let me introduce you to some friends who have conquered the situational stress.

Leslie Hale is a minister. But his church is located in Belfast, Ireland, right where so much violence has taken place these recent years. I met Leslie over the phone about six weeks before we met in person. My secretary said, "There's a minister trying to call you from Ireland." And it was Leslie Hale, Why did you call me, Leslie?

*Leslie:* I had received a copy of your book. *Move Ahead with Possibility Thinking.* As I read it, I got excited. I felt that you were doing more for God accidently than most people do purposefully. Especially in my country where everything is negative and depressing, with the violence and the trouble. So I decided I had to talk with you, to be inspired and to be positive, because we are about to launch out and build a large church. It will be the largest church ever to be built in Ireland for both Catholics and Protestants. Our ministry is to both because we just try to turn people on to the Lord Jesus Christ.

*Dr. Schuller:* As soon as I answered the phone, you said, ''Tell me something positive!'' I was almost speechless!

*Leslie:* Well, I'm glad you weren't. You said, ''Take down these four points. And I wrote them down. As a result of that telephone call, I'm here in Garden Grove today and have just finished the Institute for Successful Church Leadership sessions. It's been fantastic.

*Dr. Schuller:* It's been a thrill to have you here. You know, the week after you called, I delivered a message called, ''The Miracle of Thinking Big.'' I said if a big idea comes into your mind, and if it's a good idea, a clean idea and a God-given idea, then act on it. And that's what you did. Tell us about your church.

*Leslie:* We've already started because we

believed the Lord would give us the money we needed for the land. We prayed for 10,000 pounds, which, at that time, was about $24,000. But we also prayed that God would give us that much money in one night, in cash, and in the center of town. Now that is a ludicrous thing to normally think about. But we not only prayed that way, we announced in the press that God would give us the money. In Belfast, that's like expecting the moon to fall into your backyard.

So we rented a large auditorium and drove through some of the violence to get there. When we arrived, there were 1500 people there! The British Army and the police were also there with their machine guns to guard the offering. So they must have believed us! It took ten men, one hour and five minutes to count the offering. We collected it in a large barrel. The television people and the newspaper people were all there watching. When I came out and announced that we had received $35,000 in cash, pandemonium broke out. And all that right in the middle of Belfast.

*Dr. Schuller:* That's tremendous. It was a privilege to pray with you about that offering. You told me something about the land you bought. It was ten acres, right?
*Leslie:* Yes, we bought ten acres in a beautiful area right by the freeway. We have rented a big tent and we're going to start to build soon. It will

be the largest church ever built in Ireland and will seat 2,000 people. It will be for the Catholics and the Protestants, because all the violence is not between Catholics and Protestants. I don't think many people understand that. There are guerilla groups operating, but the vast majority of Catholics and Protestants love each other and just want the violence to end.

*Dr. Schuller:* I think another amazing miracle took place about the zoning problems you encountered.

*Leslie:* We bought the land even though it had been turned down for re-zoning for religious purposes. I went back to the city fathers and said, "You've made a mistake. You have to change your mind. God told me to build this church on that land!" And amazingly, they re-zoned it.

*Dr. Schuller:* I suppose that could only happen in Ireland—or any place a possibility thinker moves out on faith!

Leslie faces tremendous pressures and stress in terms of the dangers to his life and his family. But God gives him strength to move ahead. Dwight Dobson works under different conditions. I met him when I visited Calcutta several years ago. He is living proof of the fact that if you have a lot of love at the center of your faith, your faith will never give up, and you will not fail. I suppose having a black belt in judo helped a little also, didn't it Dwight?

*Dwight:* It did, but the story goes way back to when I was a little boy. I was raised as a preacher's kid. At a very early age, my parents encouraged me to give my heart and life to Jesus Christ.

I always enjoyed the missionaries coming to our home. But I'd always get booted out of my room so they would have a place to sleep. I finally got a little book and registered everybody's name who slept in my bed. I look back often these years and I can see some of the influence these people had on my life.

*Dr. Schuller:* Was it at that time you decided to be a missionary?

*Dwight:* I began to feel an impulse in that direction. I believed God wanted me to follow that calling. Every job I have ever had has been with one thought in mind—one day I would be a missionary.

*Dr. Schuller:* When did you become interested in judo?

*Dwight:* In elementary school, I became fascinated as I watched on television the bodies flying through the air with the greatest of ease. And in my mind I said, "When I get big I would like to learn how to do that." I discovered that our high school had a judo club. So when I started high school, judo was my sport. And in a very short time I was a black belt. In my senior year, 7 out of the 10 on our state judo team were from our high school. We came out here to California and tied for third place in the nation that year.

Everything was going right as far as I was concerned. After I finished college I felt it was the time to apply to go overseas. Dr. Mark Buntain, who works in Calcutta, contacted me and said, "Dwight, would you come to Calcutta?" My wife and I prayed about it and we sensed all the lights were green—Go to Calcutta!

In six months I had raised my support and applied to the Indian government for a visa. They wrote back and said I had insufficient education. Within a week I was back in college and jammed in 25 units in one semester. When I finished, I applied again. This time they simply said no.

Down deep inside we still felt Calcutta was the place we would end up. The Lord said, "Keep trusting me, I'm guiding you and leading you." Since we couldn't go to Calcutta, we went to Ceylon for a year. That was as long as we were allowed to stay. We planned on going to Beirut, Lebanon next. I wrote to Pastor Buntain in Calcutta and told him we were going to Beirut. He fired a letter back to me and said, "Dwight, don't you dare fly over! Come to Calcutta and we're going to try one more time to get you a visa." We did.

Six weeks later I stood in a policeman's office as he pulled my file from the case. He said, "Reverend, your file is full of rejections. There's no possible way you can come to India and be a missionary. Now your visitors visa is due tomorrow, so please leave."

I wondered why. Finally I told the Lord it was His burden that He gave us about Calcutta. So if He didn't want us there now, maybe He meant later. I went down to buy the tickets for Beirut. We were scheduled to leave at 10:00 on Thursday morning.

Wednesday night I had promised some boys I would give a demonstration at their judo club. When I returned home, Anita, my wife, and our oldest son were sick in bed. Now it isn't very easy to travel part way around the world when you're sick. But I told them to get better because if we didn't make the flight we would loose half of our fare. When I went to bed, I prayed for a miracle—like having the Lord change the wording on the tickets or help my family to feel well enough to travel. But when morning came, nothing had changed. The tickets were the same and my family was still sick.

As the minutes clicked by, I used every means of persuasion to get them out of bed, and into a taxi. But Calcutta's not a place to travel when you don't feel well. Finally, I sat down on the side of the bed and agreed, "We're not going today."

I sat there and pouted. About fifteen minutes later, the phone rang. I walked over, picked it up, and the gentleman on the other end of the line said, "Rev. Dobson, please." I said, "Speaking." The voice continued, "I'm the deputy commissioner of Calcutta police. Please stay where you are. I anticipate being at your residence in fifteen minutes." I had my first symptoms of heart trouble as I hung up the phone, I assure you.

It seemed like forever, but fifteen minutes later the deputy commissioner knocked on our door. After he sat down, he said, "Rev. Dobson, the communists have taken over our State through the recent elections. They have brought a subversive group into our community." I nodded as he related the recent bombings, muggings and killings on the streets. "They chased out of our city over 1,500 businesses. And they have put bounties on the heads of the police. Kill a policeman and you get 200 rupees. Kill a commissioner and you get 20,000 rupees."

My nervousness started to lessen as he talked more about the problems of Calcutta and said nothing about my overstaying my visa. Finally he came to the point. "Sir, for one month I have had orders to train 20,000 policemen in judo and unarmed combat and I can't find one person in this city who would dare to stand up and give me their help. Reverend Dobson, would you stay in Calcutta and train my policemen?"

I nearly jumped clear off the chair. I had to ask him if he was serious. He repeated himself, "Sir, I have an order to give you anything you need if you will help train these policemen. Will you stay in Calcutta?"

I stood up and answered, "For three years I have tried to come to India. I have done everything your government has asked me to do and I still can't get a visa." He interrupted me, "Rev. Dobson, if I get you a visa, will you stay?" My response was immediate, "What time tomorrow morning do you want me to begin?"

"What do you need?" he asked. "Give me your ten best men," I told him. "Alright," he agreed, "they're yours. What time do you want to start?" I told him 5:00 in the morning because I didn't want him to change his mind. I was there right on time! He gave me his jeep and two bodyguards to get around the city.

About six weeks later, he came to me and said, "Rev. Dobson, I would like to think that because you're a Christian that you might want to spend about five minutes every day telling the policemen you train about your faith and why you are in India." I gulped and before I could answer, he added, "Go ahead, the privilege is yours."

*Dr. Schuller:* Amazing! Are you still involved in that training?

*Dwight:* Yes, they just finished building a large gym for me to train the policemen in. I've also had the joy of being the head coach of the state team and I was asked to be the head coach of India's Olympic judo team for the games in Munich and Montreal.

*Dr. Schuller:* What words of encouragement would you give to someone who may be caught in circumstances they don't understand?

*Dwight:* As a little boy praying in my daddy's church, God planted within my heart the desire for the sport of judo. Judo has taken me to the President's palace of India, 7,500 feet up in the Himalayan Mountains. I've been in the Governor's mansion and in the emergency room of the Calcutta Police Hospital. And every place I have been able to take the name of Jesus and share Him—for His praise and for His glory. So be patient, and keep your eyes on Jesus. He's in control!

I don't have to spend too much time training policemen today. So I also work in a church of about 2,000. I participate in the seven services we have on Sunday. We have a day school for Jesus with 1,400 kids enrolled. We're feeding 1,600 children every day. In the last 15 years we've fed over a million mouths. We're building a brand new hospital with 100 beds to share the needs of that city. And all along the way I say,"Thank you, Jesus, that in a little boy's life you put the ability in my hands to share your name."

*Dr. Schuller:* Thank you Dwight, you're still the only man I hesitate to shake hands with.

Circumstances can be overwhelming, especially when they are caused by the color of your skin. There are many examples of men and women who have conquered racial prejudice. But I don't know a better example than my good friend, Jester Hairston. There isn't a high school music director — in fact, there isn't a director of any choir in any college or university in America that doesn't know the name Jester Hairston. He is unquestionably the foremost arranger and composer of classical Negro music. Jester, you're a legend in your own lifetime.

*Jester:* Thank you, Dr. Schuller. It's a privilege for me to count you as one of my friends.

*Dr. Schuller:* You grew up in a Christian home, didn't you?

*Jester:* I sure did, I just did work at being a Christian when I was young. I left home when I was twelve. So I had enough religion at that age to carry me through the rest of life. I never did go back home, but my grandmother and my mother laid the foundations of faith that made the difference in my life.

*Dr. Schuller:* How did you become a musician?

*Jester:* I was planning on being a farmer. My first two years in college were spent in the University of Massachusetts, which was an agricultural college. I was studying farming and horticulture. I met a lady in Amhurst, Massachusetts — a white lady — who became my accompaniest. I sang, but I didn't know anything about music and didn't really care. I just sang for fun. But she became interested in my musical abilities and said, "I think you ought to go to Boston and study music seriously." I replied, "I don't have the money or the interest." "You can be of more benefit to your race and to the country as a whole in music than you can as a farmer," she told me. This lady was a school teacher and school teachers back there in the early 20's were not making very much. But she took all her savings and sent me to Boston. I studied music there and then went on to New York.

*Dr. Schuller:* Perhaps your farming background is the reason your work is so fruitful. Having been born in Iowa, I have an excuse for my corny material. Jester, of all the honors that have come into your distinguished life, what is one of the most touching things that you have experienced?

*Jester:* Oh, I have had many, many touching experiences. I think one of the greatest experiences I've had is the opportunity that my country has given me. I've loved people all my life. I tell some of the young people of my own race how much prejudice there was when I was growing up. But even then I loved people. And

It's been such a wonderful opportunity to carry a message of love through music.

I can learn a certain amount of any language overnight. God has given me that ability. And in my travels to so many countries, I learn to at least say, "I'm delighted and greatly honored to bring the greetings of my country to you ladies and gentlemen." You can win people if you love them and they can see it.

*Dr. Schuller:* Have you been to Russia?

*Jester:* I was supposed to go to Russia in 1961. I studied Russian for a year in preparation for my trip. I had a private teacher come to my home to teach me. Then a week before I was supposed to go, Brother Kruschev called up brother Kennedy and said, "Niet." So I didn't go. They sent me to Germany instead. I've been to Germany so many times and have so many friends there.

*Dr. Schuller:* Jester, you've conquered the stress of racial prejudice. What words of encouragement would you give to someone still fighting that battle?

*Jester:* You have prejudice within all races and against each other. I've gone to certain countries that have said they could understand my spirituals which describe the troubles Blacks have experienced. They can understand because they have lived through the same troubles. In one county in Europe they said, "Another country had us under its heel for over a hundred years, so we can understand what you sing about.''

My solution is love. You have to practice love. You can't just say, ''I am a Christian and I love.'' The love has to come from your heart and control your understanding. I know some black people who think all white people stink. And I know whites who think the same about blacks. Well now, you get someone like that and you'll have a rough time trying to inspire that person to be civilized. But I think love will slowly win the battle.

It's coming in this country. I'll be conducting in a white Southern Baptist Church in Georgia. Ten years ago, or maybe even less, I wouldn't be permitted to even walk in front of that church because I'm black. But now I'm going to be there as a conductor. I'll be in charge! I did the same thing recently in the largest white Southern Baptist Church in Dallas, Texas and they treated me wonderfully.

*Dr. Schuller:* Jester, the key is your love. And the key to your love is there's somebody that came into your heart a long time ago and His name is . . .

*Jester:* Jesus!

*Dr. Schuller:* Thank you, Jester.

I recently had the privilege of interviewing three special people on our program. All three are from Uganda. Festo Kivengere is a Bishop in the Church of Uganda and was a close friend of the Archbishop who was martyred by President Amin. In fact, Festo's life was endangered and he barely escaped the country. With him is Adoniya Kirinda, who is a student at Fuller Theological Seminary and his mother, who just arrived in this country from Uganda. Festo, you had to flee your country. When was that?

*Festo:* I left the country of Uganda right after the death of the Archbishop. The Archbishop was martyred for his stand for Jesus Christ and afterwards a number of us were sought by Amin's soldiers. But the Lord led my wife and me to safety.

*Dr. Schuller:* We were praying for you in this church because we knew you were targeted for martyrdom. In fact, there were rumors that you had been killed. We rejoice with you in your escape. What has really happened to your country?

*Festo:* The very disturbing news is that once a regime takes it upon itself to use force to eliminate unwanted enemies, it has no ability to stop the harassment. But on the other side, the sunny side, the news is absolutely fantastic. Even immediately after the Archbishop had died, you read about the tremendous upsurge of spiritual life. The cathedral where he would have been buried was packed out with 4,500

Christians rejoicing and singing together. I have heard that the churches are growing faster than ever. The response to the gospel of our Savior is tremendous. People are singing and praising Jesus because He is the only one that remains the life of Uganda.

*Dr. Schuller:* How many Christians are there in Uganda?

*Festo:* Out of a total population of eleven-and-a-half million, there are over eight million Christians. And the number is increasing every day!

*Dr. Schuller:* Festo, how did you escape?

*Festo:* God planned it all. On Saturday, my wife and I became aware that we were going to be eliminated. We looked to Jesus to make a way of escape, and you know He even makes a way in the wilderness. God's people were like angels along the way, so that even in the night when we were tracking our way through the mountains of our country there were lovely people who helped us through. They knew the way. It was wonderful.

*Dr. Schuller:* Mr. Karinda is a seminary student and we have enjoyed having him and his family with us. In fact, our church has kind of adopted all of you. Tell us about the telegram you received.

*Mr. Karinda:* It told about my mother. She was in church on Sunday morning when the soldiers came and attacked the pastor. Then they attacked my mother and imprisoned her for two days. Friends got her out of prison and helped her to hide. That's when we received the cable. We prayed and then passed it on to this church. And you did the rest.

*Dr. Schuller:* She arrived here in America yesterday. She's asking you a question, isn't she?

*Mr. Karinda:* My mother just asked me a question I can't answer. She said "How come people I have never met would send money for my escape when I was deep in the heart of Africa hiding?" She says she is sorry for crying. I told her the only reason I can think of is the love of Jesus Christ.

*Dr. Schuller:* It is indeed. Because Jesus Christ lives in our hearts we are all members of the family of God.

*Mr. Karinda:* She says, "I want you to know that my heart is full of thanksgiving for that kind of action of love. Apart from that loving action I would never be here. Those whose love helped me in Africa did not have the ability and funds to give me the kind of help to get me here. I praise God for His help which has produced an unbroken chain from here to Africa which joins us together as brother and sister."

Fortunately, we do not all face the horrible circumstances that Bishop Festo Kivengere and his people have faced. The church in Uganda is facing unbelievable stress, and yet with God's help they are stronger today than ever!

When circumstances weigh you down, and they will at times, be strengthened by the tremendous power of God that is within you. You do not have to be controlled by circumstances. Events do not direct your activities. With God's help, you are in control. Take charge with the attitude that you will be victorious in this and every situation. I say this with confidence because:

> God is our refuge and strength, a tested help in times of trouble. And so we need not fear even if the world blows up, and the mountains crumble into the sea! (Psalm 46:1,2 TLB).

# 9

# You Can Experience Strength and Happiness

# You Can Experience Strength and Happiness

I want to give you a formula that will guarantee success to you in your search for strength and happiness. Every person we have met in the preceeding chapters has discovered this formula. And it is possible for you to find the strength to conquer the stress you are experiencing. Here is the key:

*Discover the consciousness that God is in ultimate control of your life and that His will is unfolding as it should.*

There you have it: The cure for stress! Your search is fulfilled when you develop the awareness that God is in control of your life. He has a dream for you and it is always constructive, never destructive. His plan for you is positive, which means that if you are walking close to God, you will experience strength and happiness. If you do encounter stress, you can know that it is only a phase, where God is either: (1) delaying, (2) guiding, (3) redirecting, (4) expanding your thinking, or (5) making you so humble that when joy and strength come it won't go to your head.

What can you do during times of stress? There are four words that rhyme that illustrate four simple points to help you. The words are *Pray, Obey, Pay and Stay.*

You begin with *Prayer.* "God, I want your will to be done in my life." Now some people create a lot of inner stress because they are unwilling to pray that prayer. They don't want to take this first step. They have an idea of what they want, and God is only somebody that they may want to use to get their own way. Prayer is not some device to get heaven to move to earth so that you can get what you want.

I've used this illustration before because it makes the point so clearly. If you're in a little boat approaching a sandy beach and you throw out the anchor, it digs into the sand. When you pull on the anchor rope until the boat slides onto the shore, what have you done? Have you moved the shore to the boat? Or have you moved the boat to the shore? Obviously you have pulled the boat to the shore. The purpose of prayer, likewise, is not to move God and heaven to you, but to move you closer to God so that you want what God wants.

*Pray.* Pray that you will be open to what God wants you to do. Pray that you will hear God speaking to you in the center of the storm of stress.

After you have prayed, then *obey* positive signals. Some people never find strength or personal happiness because frankly, they are harboring secret sins. They're not living right, they're not living clean, and they know it. Because they are not obeying God, they are not able to receive strength and power in their life. They can't hear God's messages to them because they are not within calling distance. Until you are obeying God you won't want to get close to Him, because you'll be afraid with your guilt. Take the time to search your conscience and determine to remove any secret sin that you find.

If you have prayed and are willing to obey, then determine to *pay* the price. In the Christian life there is always some sacrificing involved. Jesus Christ couldn't accomplish His task without the cross. And there will be some point where we must be willing to deny ourselves and pay the price. In order for you to find strength, you may have to pay the price of stress for a while. Be confident! God is with you!

That leads into the last point. *Stay* with God. Don't quit. What you may need is patience.

Strength and happiness are just ahead. Keep trusting God. Keep believing! Never give up! *God's delays are not God's denials.* Your life is unfolding exactly as it should. How do I know that? God has promised!

> *"In everything you do, put God first, and he will direct you and crown your efforts with success"* (Proverbs 3:6 TLB).

> *"I will instruct you (says the Lord) and guide you along the best pathway for your life; I will advise you and watch your progress"* (Psalm 32:8 TLB).

> *"God shows how to distinguish right from wrong, how to find the right decision every time. For wisdom and truth will enter the very center of your being, filling your life with joy"* (Proverbs 2:9, 10 TLB).

> *"You saw me before I was born and scheduled each day of my life before I began to breathe. Every day was recorded in your Book!"* (Psalm 139:16 TLB).

> *"I have created you and cared for you since you were born. I will be your God through all your lifetime, yes, even when your hair is white with age. I made you and I will care for you. I will carry you along and be your Savior"* (Isaiah 46:3,4 TLB).

The most powerful force in the world is a positive attitude in the mind of a believer who is walking close to God!